MARK FISHER

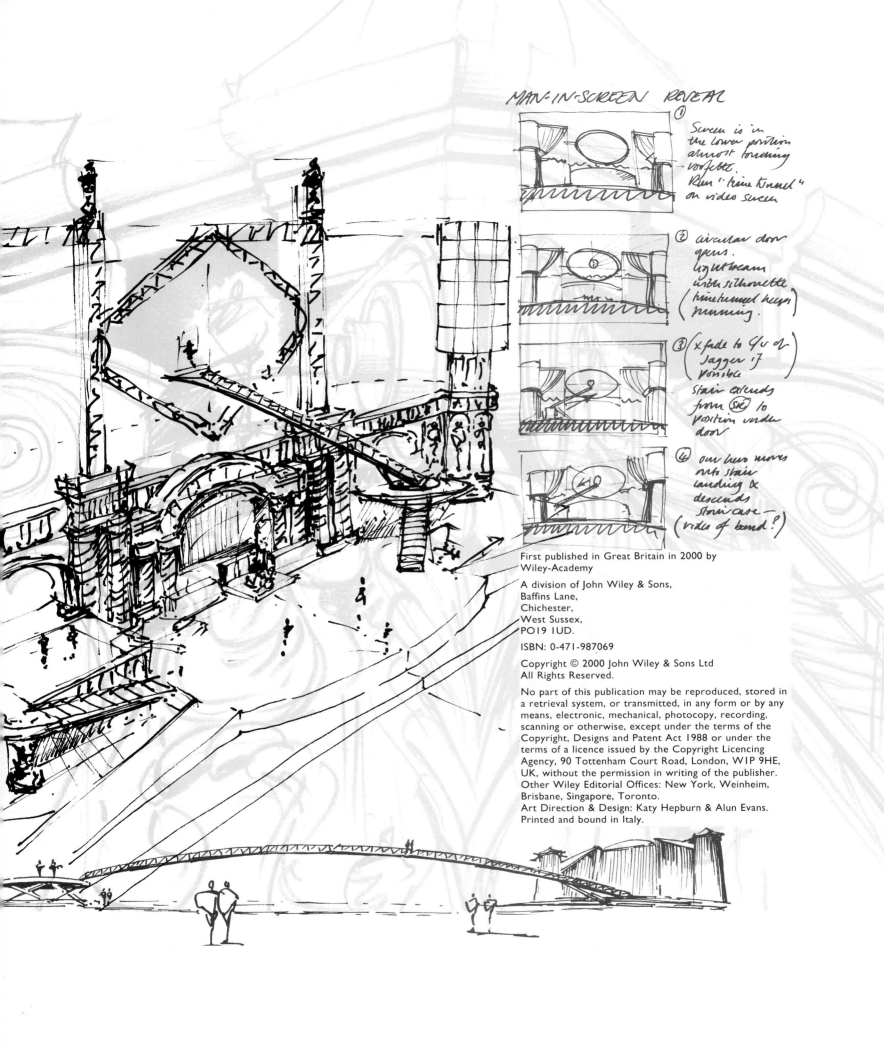

MAN-IN-SCREEN REVEAL

① Screen is in the lower position almost touching verticle. Run "time tunnel" on video screen

② circular door opens. light beam with silhouette (time tunnel helys) running.

③ (x fade to Clu of Jagger ?) visible stair extends from (SK) to position under door

④ our hero moves onto stair landing & descends staircase — (video of band ?)

First published in Great Britain in 2000 by
Wiley-Academy

A division of John Wiley & Sons,
Baffins Lane,
Chichester,
West Sussex,
PO19 1UD.

ISBN: 0-471-987069

Other Wiley Editorial Offices: New York, Weinheim,
Brisbane, Singapore, Toronto.
Art Direction & Design: Katy Hepburn & Alun Evans.
Printed and bound in Italy.

ERIC HOLDING

MARK FISHER
STAGED ARCHITECTURE

Architectural Monographs No 52

WILEY-ACADEMY

Contents

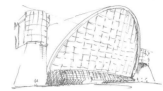

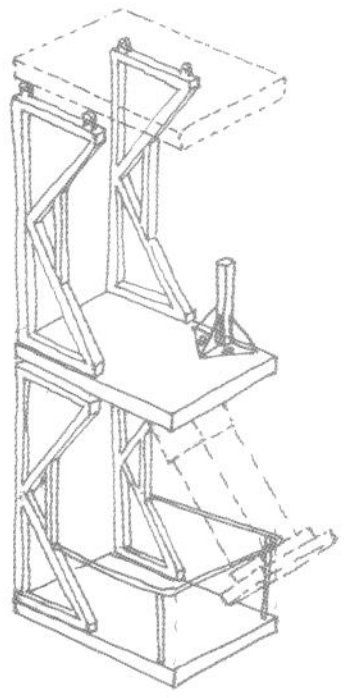

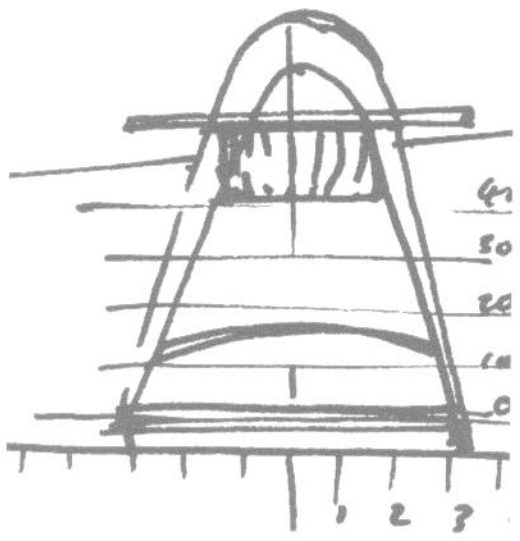

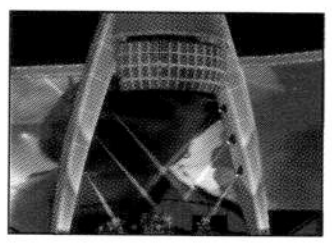

62

88

102

125

128

Bridges to Babylon

Logistics

Popmart

Aftermath

Playlist

Acknowledgments

I took this invitation for my work to be published in an AD Monograph as an opportunity to place it in the contemporary cultural context. The steelwork may be rooted in the industrial age technologies of transport and manual assembly, but the decoration is based in the post-industrial world of commodification and brand management. I was impressed by what Eric Holding and Sarah Chaplin achieved in editing and writing *Consuming Architecture*, and I thought Eric would make a good job of decoding the role of this placeless architecture in our consumer-led society.

I think his review will come as a surprise to many of those whom I must thank for making the work shown here possible: The bands - Pink Floyd, U2 and the Rolling Stones - whose commercial self interest has been well served by these projects but who still had to pay for them out of their own pocket. The production managers - Michael Ahern, Jake Berry, Jake Kennedy, and Robbie Williams - who shouldered day by day responsibility for the logistical performance of these projects against timetables which would make the building industry weep with incredulity. The lighting designers and show directors - Marc Brickman, Willie Williams and Patrick Woodroffe - with whom I have collaborated on these projects; I hope they can see through Eric's prose and understand that I recognise how their contribution to these shows often exceeded my own. The crews and contractors - in the end it was they who built it all - who erected each of these stages over 100 times in less than a year.

Some of the work included here was created while I was in partnership with Jonathan Park. Together we designed Steel Wheels, The Wall in Berlin, ZooTV, and Voodoo Lounge. I would like to thank him for the great time we shared. Today my studio is virtually almost to the point of invisibility; the still frames included here are from hours of video animation by Adrian Mudd.

I would like to thank the buiders: Tony Bowern, Richard Hartman, Charlie Kail, Hedwig de Meyer and Michael Tait, the engineers: Mal McLaren and Neil Thomas, and my assistants: Adrian Mudd, Gillian Whiting and Ray Winkler for all the help they have given me on these projects. I would like to thank David Greene for writing the introduction. And I would like to thank Katy Hepburn and Alun Evans for designing the book.

Mark Fisher

I would like to extend my personal thanks to the following individuals: Firstly, to Mark who despite spending the majority of his life on airplanes always made time for discussion, during which more ideas emerged regarding the rock concert as a cultural phenomenon than all of the academic research I carried out. For other insights I am indebted to some of Mark's collaborators, in particular Patrick Woodruffe and Willie Williams.

I would like to thank Katy Hepburn and Alun Evans for their remarkable graphic design and Martin Tothill for capturing the atmosphere of Mark's studio on film. Thanks also go to Barry Curtis, Director of Research and Professor of Visual Culture at Middlesex University for the time and funding to develop this project.

Finally, I would like to mention my wonderful parents, Chris and Dorothy Holding, who put up with me listening to (loud) rock music as a teenager and yet missed out on the quiet bit when I was writing about it, and the rest of my family for their support including Ann-Louise, Neil, Lynne, Lynsey and Christopher, Bob and Davina, Heidi and Robin, and Beryl.

Most of all I would like to thank my wife, Sarah Chaplin, who played a significant role in the editing of this book, and is a constant source of inspiration and encouragement. You complete me. Our first child is due to arrive in the world at the same time as this book, and whoever you are, little one, this is for you.

Eric Holding

Ice Cream Man
by David Greene

Summer 1998. An email from Fisher asking me to contribute to a book on his work. 'I know how scornful you are of these things, but then it is your rapier wit and cynical vision that I seek.' (MF 98/07/07, 04:03) The internet makes geography invisible. Only the timestamp hints at location. 'Are you anxious to legitimise your career by support acts from the word industry?' (DG 98/07/16, 20:13) 'The book will be nothing more than another piece of vanity publishing masquerading as an intellectual review of the pop-consumer fin-de-millennium position. I am currently in Yokohama working with a Japanese rock god who lies on his back on the stage waving his legs in the air and playing the guitar with his teeth.' (MF 98/07/17, 02:41) Typically blunt, and mired in trivia, Fisher was in Japan.

July 22nd 1999, 10.50 p.m. On Channel 4, Mark Morrison gives a fair impression of aggression, a mixed-race gang of good-looking girls and boys performing against a psychedelic background reminiscent of San Francisco in 1965. The song Crazy completes the time warp. Terry Christian leers out of the screen inviting viewers to watch Best of the Word again next week. I flick to another channel, avoiding the Great Ford Summer Drive (cute graphics of hyper-red strawberries drifting against a white ground) and zap a video on the website of the model Caprice, singing her new single against another psychedelic background reminiscent of San Francisco 1965. This banal scene, the background noise of recycled media, is the real site of Fisher's work: an environment of images and sound. His architecture is grounded in this post-literate culture; its success can be measured only by its power to communicate. 'The rock set is ultimately placeless, like a T-shirt.' (DG email 98/08/19, 19:17) This is architecture as wallpaper, a wardrobe for the audience.

In 1964 Marshall McLuhan observed that as culture becomes increasingly structured and configured by new media systems, 'concern with *effect* rather than *meaning* is a basic change of our electric time.' If we see Fisher's work in this context, then we cannot deny the power of its effect. But if we regard McLuhan's assertion as a criticism then we must con-

clude that his work is meaningless - not that this would perturb him - 'I like the contradiction implicit in selling artistic integrity as a commodity.' (MF 99/07/11, 10.03)

Buckminster Fuller, Cedric Price and Marshall McLuhan must have been major influences on Fisher as a student. At one level his work is a fusion of their ideas. The question asked by Buckminster Fuller (How much does your building weigh?), the assertion of Cedric Price (It is as important to know how to take your building down as to put it up), and McLuhan's claim that electric light is space without walls - all these are bread and butter to Fisher; they are his media. His architecture is short-term rental, not long-term freehold. As fast as it is built on one site, somewhere else in the night its double is cruising down the freeway. Like Best of the Word, sometimes it's there but when it's gone only memories remain.

Can we see the work in this book as a marker on the way to bypassing the exhausted games of the architectural form factories? Its geographical rootlessness challenges architecture itself, which is wedded to ideas of the authentic, not only conceptually but also literally in terms of site. Like clothing, lightweight and portable, Fisher's work needs a host to attach itself to, but in the end it is placeless.

Back to his request. I suggested that he should know better than to try to pander to a derelict culture of academic legitimisation when his work ought to be part of the street and not the library. Was this the Fisher I knew, whose hair corkscrewed to the sky, whose clipped and abbreviated sentences made Clint Eastwood seem almost garrulous, whose ambling gait made me wonder if he had a former life as a cowboy, someone who saw rock 'n' roll as 'the ultimate low-rent blue-collar myth of twentieth century cowboys getting the girls'? (MF 99/07/11, 10:30) Maybe cowboy is ok. Or pirate?

In his writing about the Temporary Autonomous Zone (TAZ), Hakim Bey offers the pirate as a utopian paradigm of the contemporary world: mobile, resourceful and networked. 'Temporary Autonomous Zones live high off the surplus of over production, they exist with an air of impermanence, of being ready to move, to shape, to shift, to relocate to other planes of reality... a guerrilla operation which liberates an area of land, of time, of imagination, and then dissolves itself....'

I wanted to see the events Fisher designs as spontaneous and as nomadic TAZs, but they are more like the work of an army than a pirate ship. Although the origins of rock 'n' roll are rooted in the anti-establishment protests of the sixties, the rock business has always been compromised by commercial self-interest. As Kevin Rhowbotham points out, the real pirates of the 60's were interested in 'an architecture of event which concentrated on the production of situations rather than mute lithic mass ...a latent urbanism in which the city could be reconfigured by an act of mind. ...The squat, the street demonstration, the rave, are its legacy.' The manifesto of the Situationist International, one of the prime forces behind the Paris Riots of 1968, demanded the same degree of anarchic political commitment and sponteneity as Hakim Bey: a condition that was quickly diluted. Rhowbotham also reminds us that 'at the hands of the contemporaneous and de-politicised avant-garde ...Archigram, Haus Rucker, Coop Himmelblau, Superstudio, et al., the SI's protean architecture of events suffered a chic reversal of its political intentions. ...this gamut of self-styled poseurs and gallery traders abandoned the radical teleology of the SI's position.' Fisher's work forms a natural development of the sixties avant-garde precisely because it is so unspontaneous.

Fisher knows well that his work operates in a highly commercial world. Rock concerts are simulated tribal gatherings, manufactured to promote a band and simultaneously cater to a contemporary need for real (as opposed to virtual) experience. They are as unauthentically spontaneous as the 'events' in the plaza in front of the Pompidou Centre, synthetic spectacles for the consumption of the temporary nomad we call the tourist. But unlike the contrived street theatre of Beaubourg, at least Fisher admits his provenance. He knows how much his architecture costs and weighs, and he knows how to take it down and get it on the road. As a dreamer I like to imagine these structures of effects and social gathering as

prototypes, models for an architecture which is different from the kind the magazines promote, something more ephemeral, something that lands on the earth lightly, something that shimmers.

I return again to his original e-mail. There was a note of caution in the invitation to write this introduction; in particular, had I lost my venom? If I hadn't, I might have replied, 'your work is not art, and it's not architecture. It's just a neat trick in the service of parting people from their money'. I wondered why he even wanted to call it architecture. 'Why not? It's about creating space in time. Anyway, computer designers have already appropriated the word 'architecture'. It won't be long before they call themselves architects.' (MF 98/08/19, 17:47) Which brought us to Buckminster Fuller's famous remark about 'invisible know-how'; that none of the technical research and development which will affect our future is 'directly apprehendible by any of the human senses.' 'This is absolutely wrong. The diminishing cost of transportation is one 20C development that can be seen and experienced. The transportation of goods used to be one of the largest invisible factors governing the form, appearance and permanence of buildings. But the cost of transporting raw materials and finished products has changed from significant to trivial in less than 100 years. It is the reason why large-scale rock concerts are economically feasible.' (MF 98/08/20, 03:56)

There is much in Fisher's work that connects to persistent mid-twentieth century theoretical themes: nomadism, time, event, the road, short-life architecture, light and sound as the material of architecture. I am wondering about Archigram: what residue of its work remains? Should I draw connections to projects like the 'Ideas Circus', where links to Fisher's events seem so obvious. 'There is an ironic connection between some of the propositions of Archigram which excited me at the AA, based as they were on an optimistic reading of the most extravagant technology man has ever invented, and their eventual low tech realisation in the nomadic world of rock 'n' roll. I enjoy the contradiction between how we thought it would be back in the 60's and how it turned out, both

technologically and culturally. (Streamlined, multinational-corporation style popular culture delivered with cheap and primitive technology, as opposed to the high-tech delivery of hang-loose politically charged free expression happenings).' (MF 98/07/17, 10:55) The big difference between theory and practice is that Fisher's work is all performed within a theatre of money. 'These sets form a sort of Baroque phase of performance, a frightening condition whereby the machinery of promotion and exploitation attempts to devour the audience'. (DG 98/08/19, 19:17) In spite of its ephemeral qualities, the work in this book is similar to the fin-de-siecle position of the giant out-of-town shopping temples, which camouflage retailing as entertainment in a last gasp before it drowns in cyberspace.

In Fisher's work we find an overt pursuit of effect. The structural technology is hardly cutting-edge; 'the average rock tour is about as high-tech as the building of the pyramids.' (MF 98/07/16, 02:41) And his tirades against 'pseudo-technology' - particularly that of Hi-Tech buildings - are familiar to his fans. He claims 'it is one of the duties of the architect to be as economical as possible. Both the Romans and Barratt homes understand this very well, sourcing the most basic materials for the primary construction and then applying a veneer of culture to the most visible surfaces.' (MF email 98/07/17, 10:55) Fisher has applied some pretty exotic techno-fluff to his primitive armatures. But he dismisses it all: 'The economic forces which drive rock shows include a search for novelty... so there is pressure amongst show designers to seek out and employ any new technology that is around.' (MF 1999/08/10, 09:46)

But what about 'concern with *effect* rather than *meaning*'. McLuhan went on to say that '...effect involves the total situation'. It brings us to a recurring theme in Fisher's thinking: the phenomenon of branding. Unlike signature architects, whose buildings are personally branded fashion products like Armarni suits, Fisher brands in a temporary and impersonal way. His architectural style is self-consciously plastic, manipulated to suit the brand values of his clients. 'I try to achieve a level of colloquial directness in my work. Because my clients must maintain very close relationships with their audiences, I have to maintain a good understanding of their different values and sign systems. Signature architects do this too, it's just that they don't like to admit it. When the MCC buys an old transistor radio for a press box, they are obviously not buying a functional building, they are buying a symbol which co-opts high-tech transportation imagery for a garden shed application. The general public are intended to read the building as a sign that cricket is not a boring 200 year old game, but some zappy close relative of Formula One.' (MF 99/080/10, 09:09)

Rock concert audiences are presented with quasi-rituals, oven-ready lifestyles; like shopping malls the stadia become post-modern sites of happy consumption. Media recycling makes experience a saleable commodity and allows the machinery of consumer rock 'n' roll to make a living, but more importantly it gives it a grand, lyrical, spectacular, poetic (but momentary) physical presence in an ephemeral post-modern culture. These events and temporary architectural decorations form one element of a complex system of branding. It's all straightforward stuff: Merchant Ivory, Pink Floyd, just flip a channel, the book of the film of the web-site of the CD of the T-shirt of the live performance. Structurally speaking, it's all the same, and it multiplies as technology relentlessly fragments the authority of originality until even these live performances and the architecture itself become a kind of advertising. As McLuhan anticipated, this is the condition of late twentieth century culture: style conquers all; ideas are continuously recycled into a market that never reaches a state of repletion.

Where do Fisher's creations lie in this condition of frenzied image reiteration and simulation? If we think of them as architecture, we inevitably think about space, in the sense of Plato's definition of space as enclosure. But Fisher achieves his enclosure by light, sound and image, so space becomes a place where something happens, a temporary territorial event much more akin to a depoliticised TAZ, the space of the battle being where the battle takes place. I would argue that Fisher is the one of the few architects today whose work originates in those aspects of

culture peculiar to the late twentieth century: time and image.

Architects rarely address time, although in their geometric complexities and in their unruly forms and continuous surfaces, they may allude to change or dynamic conditions. Most built architecture remains as fixed as a Palladian villa, heavyweight objects resisting the ephemeral conditions of a wired planet. The Bilbao Guggenheim is a good example of this expressive dynamism. Despite its contorted form, it does not engage time in the way that a rock spectacle does so effectively. The container yard beside the museum is a better example of late twentieth century architecture.

If architects address image, it is usually through the pursuit of a private rather than a public language. Fisher describes his work as 'the collision between blue-collar technology (trucks, steel erectors, etc.), popular culture (clearly legible signs), and sex appeal for unemployable intellectuals.' (MF 99/07/11, 10.03a.m.) Back in the fifties Reyner Banham recognised that an essential feature of popular culture was the disposability of everything, including its aesthetic qualities. Fisher's work is both colloquial and disposable. Contemporary architecture can only engage the evanescent world of media through demolition.

It's August 19th, 1999. Back from Bilbao. 'Cruising along in my automobile', the sun setting in my rear-view mirror, the radio tuned to 94.5FM; a Koons puppy key-ring dangles from the ignition and, yes, Caprice is being interviewed again. I speculate on which is the most powerful brand image: Jeff Koons' puppy of flowers or the Gehry building itself. Both the building and the contents are an integral part of the art market. And either could become the backdrop to Caprice's next video, or Fisher's next event. The machinery of reiteration grinds inexorably. I am wondering how to finish this essay. As our mediated world moves from literate to visual, from meaning to effect, I am reminded of a review I read earlier in the summer: 'Seriously, someone should really think hard about the design of stadium sets and what they actually NEED, as opposed to what they've got into the habit of having. They're always so creaky and naff and

cumbersome and ugly, evolving into gigantism like the dinosaurs when they should be thinking lean and mean and indestructible like fleas. But why not, if they're spending all that money, get a proper artist to design something worth looking at?' Even today, forty years after McLuhan, some people just don't get it.

Marshall McLuhan 'Understanding Media' 1964
Hakim Bey: 'T.A.Z. The Temporary Autonomous Zone, Ontology Anarchy, Poetic Terrorism' 1991
Kevin Rhowbotham: 'Field Event: Field Space' 1998
Buckminster Fuller 'GRUNCH of Giants' 1983
Archigram 'Ideas Circus', 'Milanogram', Architect's Journal 29 May 1968
Reyner Banham, 'Industrial Design and Popular Art' Industrial Design March 1960
Lynn Barber: The Observer, June 13 1999, reviewing the Rolling Stones 'Bridges to Babylon' concert at Wembley Stadium.

Staged Architecture

'CLAP YOUR HANDS, MICK JAGGER COMMANDS WEMBLEY, AND 70,000 PEOPLE OBEY. IT LOOKS LIKE ONE OF THOSE MASS CALLISTHENICS DEMONSTRATIONS THE CHINESE USED TO GO FOR. YEAH YEAH YEAH WOO, HE PROMPTS IN THE MIDDLE OF 'BROWN SUGAR', AND YEAH YEAH YEAH WOO WE REPLY......... IN A SUCCESSFUL STADIUM ROCK SHOW, THE AUDIENCE BECOMES THE EVENT AS MUCH AS THE PERFORMERS OR THE SET'

from 'The armies of pleasure' review of 'Voodoo Lounge' by Salman Rushdie

Over the course of the last twenty years Mark Fisher has played a major role in shaping the rock show as a cultural phenomenon, having designed some of the most spectacular and technically innovative touring outdoor stage sets ever created. In many ways these structures operate like conventional architecture, being large material forms which serve as containers for social interaction. They also allow environmental control over the space that their inhabitants occupy, and have an aesthetic dimension that lies outside of their functional requirements. Yet whilst they consti-tute architecture in these respects, they escape this categorisation in two distinct ways.

The first of these concerns the powerful social interaction between the audience and the perform-ers that takes place in a rock show, the importance of which is highlighted by Salman Rushdie. This is not like the passive relationship experienced at a tradi-tional theatrical performance or classical symphony, but one in which the audience as a collective body takes an active role, becoming emotionally and physi-cally involved in what Fisher defines as a 'tribal event'. The task of the designer in this scenario is to fashion an environment in which this dynamic rela-tionship can be played out, creating a performance space that reinforces the message of the band and their music, and intensifies the experience of the crowd.

In Fisher's work this is achieved through the con-struction of three dimensional thematic environ-ments which are scaled to the size of sports stadia and encompass the space of the crowd. These spaces communicate with the audience by using powerful visual signifiers and symbolic codes and occupy an elusive territory somewhere between representational image and tectonic form, utilising

the strategies of both for maximum effect. This exaggerated visual language produces dramatic effects which condition the audience's experience of the performance, and for this reason these structures might be regarded as 'staged architecture'.

The concept of 'staged architecture' also embodies the second distinct characteristic of Fisher's work, the notion of time which affects his approach to design in a number of ways. The most obvious of these relates to the ephemerality of the rock show environment. Unlike conventional construction which is permanent and static, Fisher's designs have a limited lifespan, existing usually for a maximum of 18 months before they are eventually discarded and thereafter exist only as memories in the minds of those who attended the concerts, or as photographs/videos which can never quite capture the experience of the event. In this respect they are fugitive architectures which, like a circus or fairground, magically arrive, recontextualise their surroundings and then disappear quite literally into the night.

Time also plays an important role in the logistics of staging these events, amounting to what might be called the 'choreography of construction', a carefully planned sequence of erection and dismantling of these nomadic structures. This is critical, since there must be a given number of shows within the tour period to ensure that the venture is financially viable. The shows themselves also effectively revolve around the design of a segment of time, a scripted sequence of events which unfold according to a predetermined show dynamic, which takes the audience on a journey, as the physical environment before them transforms to create an appropriate atmosphere to accompany the performance of each song.

THE CONCEPT OF 'STAGED ARCHITECTURE' DESCRIBES BOTH THE REPRESENTATIONAL NATURE OF FISHER'S WORK AND THE TEMPORAL DIMENSION CRITICAL TO ITS SUCCESS

Photographs of Mark Fisher's studio by Martin Tothill

Finally, time also plays a role in the thematic content of the individual shows. Whereas architecture is essentially a ponderous form of cultural production, taking large amounts of time between inception and completion, Fisher's designs frequently progress from initial sketch to the first performance in a matter of months. Given their ephemerality this allows Fisher to respond to current cultural preoccupations in the thematic content of the shows, without the anxiety of this becoming anachronistic.

Whilst such factors help set Fisher's work apart from the architectural mainstream in terms of creativity, other aspects of his work effectively exclude him from being acknowledged within the profession for his achievements. The first of these concerns the fact that his work is inextricably linked to the commercial sector, a condition still viewed with disdain by the 'gentlemen' of the profession, despite the fact that private finance is the driving force behind the vast majority of architectural commissions. That Fisher is engaged in the field of entertainment design compounds this situation, and is linked to his most serious 'transgression', the use of popular culture as a basis for signification. The use of such visual codes means his work effectively crosses the high cultural divide and fails the protocols of 'taste', even though on closer examination Fisher's work is often concerned with subverting or parodying these forms, and playing them back to the audience as a mirror of consumer society. This more than any other factor probably accounts for the reason why, despite being experienced by between 4 to 5 million people on an average tour, Fisher's work is rarely encountered in architectural publications.

The French sociologist Pierre Bourdieu has argued that the concept of 'taste' is socially constructed, and divides people into high, middle and low brow according to their levels of 'cultural competence'. This competence is partly learned in the context of family life and also in the more structured environment of the education system. At the low brow end of the cultural spectrum, Bourdieu contends that there is a marked preference for visceral experiences that appeal directly to the body. High brow culture however is seen as more cerebral, being involved with the intellect and the establishment of aesthetic preferences. In high brow terms, art is believed to have an autonomous function, beyond use value, and has the capacity to challenge social structures and cultural practices. High brow consumers pride themselves in being able to distinguish between 'good' and 'bad' cultural production, and from their influential position within society establish themselves as guardians of taste, connoisseurs of the finer things in life.

Until relatively recently, low brow consumers were deemed comparatively crude and vulgar in their preference for the products of popular culture, lacking 'taste' and therefore an ability to discern quality or to derive 'proper' aesthetic enjoyment. Postmodern theory has worked towards the dismantling of these naturalised values and challenged the notion of taste hierarchies. Despite these efforts however, this aesthetic paradigm is still a powerful force in both the production of architecture and its criticism.

This can be observed in the way architects frequently claim high cultural ground for their 'art' and attempt to deny or supress its inherent use value. This is not only apparent in the way in which architecture is formally conceptualised and theoretically discussed, but also in the way it is drawn and photographed. Architectural publishing is suffused with images that portray new buildings before they are inhabited, devoid of the trappings of everyday life and unsullied by use. In this way architecture becomes objectified and its formal aesthetic valued above its potential for social interaction. This approach also sidesteps the unsettling issue of commerciality and the fact that all architectural production, including theory, can now be seen as a commodity, which helps position individual designers and their products within the market.

In contrast, Mark Fisher's work directly confronts the issue of creativity carried out within a commercial context, and is involved with the design of environments that have popular appeal whilst communicating new ideas. This book is not concerned with this work being assigned a higher cultural value. It seeks to investigate the range of factors that have influenced the emergence and current form of the rock show as cultural phenomenon. In this way it is hoped that it will call into question whether notions of taste and high brow aesthetics have any further role to play in the architectural debate. Such arguments are heavily weighted and tend to overshadow or disregard the significance of popular phenomena. Because of this, discussions revolving around the products of popular culture frequently begin by having to state a case for themselves within this discourse, whilst high culture is rarely called upon to justify its significance in anything except its own hermetic language.

Ultimately high culture and popular culture simply constitute two forms of production, which are not mutually exclusive but rather fulfil different needs. Indeed, Fisher frequently juxtaposes high and low brow codes in his designs for rock sets in the same way that individuals allow them to collide in the construction of their own identity: 'Yeah yeah yeah WOO' sang Jagger, and 'Yeah yeah yeah WOO' replied Salman Rushdie.

Just as Fisher's work confronts entrenched thought within architecture, so it also presents a challenge to traditional publishing. Whilst the photographs that provide the only record of these ephemeral events are powerful visual images, individually they do not adequately convey the incredible psycho-physiological charge of performance, nor do they account for the dimension of time that is critical to an understanding of Fisher's work. The graphic layout of the book by Katy Hepburn and Alun Evans attempts to overcome this situation and is intended to produce the same sense of frenzied excitement and anticipation induced by a rock concert.

The effect is more filmic than book-like and serves as a constant reminder that unlike traditional architecture Fisher's work is never static. It is a dynamic unfolding experience.

Beginnings

THE SHEA
STADIUM
CONCERT WAS
ONE OF THE
MOST EXTREME
DISPLAYS OF
BEATLEMANIA

On the evening of 15 August 1965, The Beatles arrived by helicopter at Shea Stadium, home of the New York Mets baseball team, to perform on a tiny stage in front of a vast audience of over 50,000 people. At the time the band was reaching the peak of its popularity, having recently conquered the American market and in the process registered the legendary Ed Sullivan Show's highest TV ratings when they appeared on the programme.

The Shea Stadium show generated one of the most extreme displays of so-called 'Beatlemania', a term coined by the media to describe the frenzied enthusiasm for the band that completely transcended a mere appreciation of their music. Such was the response of the crowd that in addition to the band being physically remote from the audience, the performance itself was rendered practically inaudible by the screams and shouts of over-excited fans. This was despite the fact that the band employed substantially more powerful amplification than it had previously used.

The Shea Stadium show marked a significant moment in the emergence of the rock concert as a cultural phenomenon, and it provides an opportunity to examine some of the social and technological factors that brought it into being, or played a part in its subsequent development. It was one of the first rock concerts ever to be performed in a sports stadium rather than in the more intimate spaces afforded by dance halls and movie theatres. As a consequence, it generated by far the largest audience ever seen for this type of musical event. Its spectacular success at a commercial level, which signalled the arrival of rock performance as a form of mass entertainment, was matched, however, by what would now be considered an equally remarkable failure at a technical level. This is not only apparent in the inadequate equipment that was available for use, but also in the obvious lack of knowledge regarding how the relationship between the performers and their audience might be 'staged' at this scale of operation. In short, whilst rock had emerged as a distinct musical genre and quickly generated a substantial market appeal, unlike the more established types of live entertainment such as theatrical performances or symphony concerts, it had yet to develop a specific form adapted to its audience/performer relationship.

The development of a rock audience

Whilst many accounts exist of the development of rock as a musical form, few address the equally important emergence of its audience. Although a substantial following for rock and roll music had been in existence since the 1950s, the real explosion of interest in rock music took place in the early 1960s, when the children of the post-war 'baby-boom' generation were entering their teenage years.

The 'baby boomers' were a demographic aberration, caused by the sudden surge in the birth-rate that followed the demobilisation of the armed services, and the return of these young men into family life. These children were raised during the 1950s, a golden era in the United States, but which in Britain was perhaps more widely experienced as a period of prudence and austerity. This was not only because baby boomers' parents had lived through a time of war during which conspicuous displays of consumption were regarded as morally reprehensible, but also because it was not until the early 1950s that the British Government finally brought an end to the rationing of goods. From this point, the British economy rapidly developed, as products were designed and manufactured in response to new consumer markets. These new goods initially included cars, furniture, and new technologies such as television, but also as the baby boomers became teenagers, a entirely new market appeared for products and leisure activities that were aimed directly at what was in effect the first generation of young people with a disposable income.

Dick Hebdige, writing in *Hiding in the Light* (1988), and other cultural commentators have identified how the market met the need for youth consumption after 1959 with the development of discotheques, boutiques, Wimpy bars, ten-pin bowling alleys, glossy magazines, and the products of popular music including records and live concerts. However, this account is not simply an economic explanation for the rise of the rock audience which

presents them as a passive body of consumers freely exploited by the market. He reveals that a more fundamental and complex shift was also taking place in society: namely the emergence of a clearly identifiable 'youth culture'.

This transformation has been well documented by Simon Frith in his seminal book *Sound Effects: Youth, Leisure and the Politics of Rock 'n' Roll* (1983). In this text, Frith describes how at the beginning of the 1950s the notion of 'youth' was linked to that of adolescence, which is to say that it represented a finite and transitional stage on the path of an individual to adulthood. During the 1960s, however, Frith perceives a change in attitude that resulted in the 'ideology of adolescence' being transformed into the 'ideology of youth'. In this new scheme of things, being 'young' was considered as infinitely preferable to being 'old', and represented an attitude towards life that could be maintained or exhibited irrespective of age itself.

In effect, this ideology empowered the youth of the day to resist what had previously been perceived as the unavoidable responsibilities of adulthood and to lead a hedonistic existence, which was based around a display of spontaneous, exhibitionist, sexually vigorous and emotionally unconstrained behaviour. This owed much to changing social mores and the introduction of the contraceptive pill. Frith goes as far as to suggest that this distinction, a shift in attitude towards life, is what divides the essentially asinine 'pop' records of the 1950s from the more rebellious 'rock' songs of the 1960s, with the latter exemplified by The Who's 'My Generation', and its notoriously provocative sentiment: 'Hope I die before I get old'.

Dick Hebdige identifies Colin McInnies' book *Absolute Beginners* (1959) as playing a fundamental role in promoting this ideological shift, regarding it as 'largely responsible for constructing the influential paradigm of the hedonistic, working-class teenager prepared to spend a large proportion of his or her income on leisure'. Whatever its means of dissemination, this new attitude rapidly permeated an entire generation of youth. It led them into a search for specific forms of expression through which they could construct their own identity and resulted in the development of a distinct 'youth culture'.

Given this situation, it is easy to see why rock music emerged so quickly as a cultural force, for as Frith has pointed out, it operated in the creative space between an industry 'seeking to exploit a new market', and a youth audience 'seeking a medium through which to express its experience'. This volatile mix of contradictory desires, a collision between commercial forces and individual self expression, was responsible for the scenes witnessed at the Beatles' concert at Shea Stadium, and whilst today's live performances have evolved into a more defined and spectacularised form of entertainment, it is still the rapport between the band and their audience that is responsible for a truly memorable performance.

As a child of the 'baby-boom' generation, Fisher experienced these huge changes in society at first hand. By the time he started his formal training at the Architectural Association (AA) in London in September 1965, a month after the Beatles' concert at Shea Stadium, there were clear signs that architecture itself was coming under pressure to change its ideological basis.

At this time, the AA was in the middle of one of its most creative periods, and played a significant role in the development of an alternative architectural agenda, which sought to overturn the outdated dogma of a prevailing modernist ideology. Occupying a central role in this revolutionary enterprise were members of the now legendary Archigram, a highly influential group of designers and thinkers including Warren Chalk, Peter Cook, Dennis Crompton, David Greene, Ron Herron and Michael Webb, who formed an important part of the AA's teaching staff at the time, along with other luminaries such as Cedric Price.

In his introduction to a recent publication on Archigram, the American architectural critic Michael Sorkin begins with a description of the 'British Invasion' of rock music which made a huge impact on the youth of the United States in the 1960s. He goes on to draw an interesting comparison with contemporaneous developments in the field of architecture, stating, 'In 1960, Archigram coalesced and began an inventive run that paralleled that of the Beatles including the ultimate, amicable split and the continuation of a number of solo careers. Like the Beatles, Archigram ... came together almost casually – likeminded lads with a childhood in common, a rebellious sense of purpose and a remarkable rancour towards the system that they sought to overturn.'

Sorkin's comments capture the spirit of Archigram in a historical context, but they also reveal how its energy and direction were derived from the same new attitude to life that was shaping other more obvious forms of 'youth culture'. In the face of a fiercely conservative profession, still wedded to the 'high seriousness' of modernity, Archigram

The images above from left to right: Two views of an inflatable project temporarily located in the Californian desert by Mike Davies, Alan Stanton and Chris Dawson of Chrysalis (1971). Cloud project carried out by Jeffrey Shaw of the Event Structures Research Group (1975).

attempted to shift the architectural agenda towards the notions of excitement and pleasure, proposing projects which drew on popular themes and used the latest technologies to create stimulating environments for predominantly leisure-based experiences.

For its inspiration, Archigram owed a debt of gratitude to the Independent Group of artists, who eventually founded the Institute of Contemporary Arts in London and in particular the architectural theorist Reyner Banham. Fisher and his AA contemporaries took a keen interest in the activities of the IG who had initially gained critical recognition with their 'This is Tomorrow' exhibition held at the Whitechapel Gallery in 1956. This was one of the first manifestations of Pop Art and included work by the artists Richard Hamilton and Peter Blake, which drew on popular culture for both its subject matter and technique. Pop Art is seen by many cultural commentators to have been a radical response to abstract expressionism, which was an institutionalised art form divorced from everyday experience.

The cultural theorist Barry Curtis has observed that Pop Art had a widespread influence on many other fields of creative endeavour which were united by their 'questioning of elitist values and a willingness to engage with the generic, banal, consumerist and technological sensibilities of a rapidly modernising culture'. The projects carried out by members of Archigram reflected many of these concerns, and began to replace the static and unresponsive forms of modernist architecture with more dynamic, event-based approaches which proposed the use of ephemeral structures and drew on media technologies for communication.

Such environments were not the sole invention of Archigram, however, but part of a wider movement within the creative arts which placed a greater emphasis on social interaction. These events, or 'happenings' began to occur in Europe and America during the 1960s and attempted to merge several creative disciplines, bringing together art, music, film and performance into a single 'multi-media' experience. The genre was exemplified by the events organised by Andy Warhol at the Factory in New York, which involved the abrasive music of the Velvet Underground. However, in the middle of the 'swinging sixties', London was also the location of such events, due to a youth-driven 'art school scene' which supported such occasions as the '14-Hour Technicolor Dream', which featured Pink Floyd and took place at Alexandra Palace in April 1967.

The rock festivals of the late 1960s incorporated many of the characteristics of these events (which were generally regarded as the dominion of a small 'trendy' metropolitan following), but involved a much wider youth audience. The most famous of these, the Woodstock Festival, which took place in upstate New York, 15–18 August 1969, attracted a crowd in excess of 450,000 people and became synonymous with youthful hedonism and 1960s excess. This event was an inspiration to Archigram, whose Instant City project of the same year engaged with the idea of a large temporary community and proposed a 'travelling metropolis' that 'comes to a community, giving it a taste of the metropolitan dynamic'.

The projects carried out by Archigram began to replace the static and unresponsive forms of modernist architecture with more dynamic, event-based approaches which proposed the use of ephemeral structures and communication technologies.

AUTOMAT
CHANGED SHAPE
IN RESPONSE TO
ITS USERS'
PHYSICAL
REQUIREMENTS

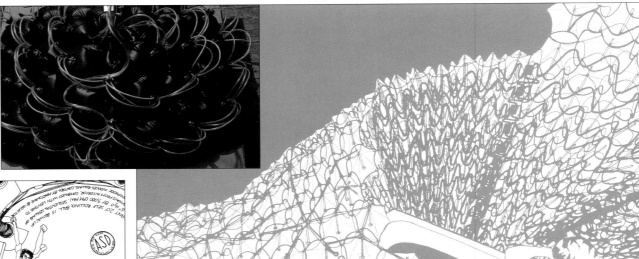

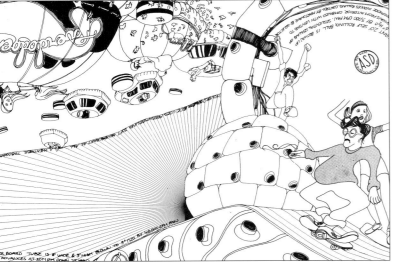

The success of Woodstock inspired many similar events such as the Isle of Wight Festival, for which Fisher helped build the stage structure designed by the engineer Anthony Hunt. Inevitably through his own direct experience of attending events like this, and given the powerful influence of Archigram, Fisher's work reflected the spirit of the times, which is apparent in his designs for an Adult Theme Park carried out in 1970. The drawings, which have a loose playful quality, depict a youthful population exercising its right to hedonistic behaviour, and inhabiting an artificial entertainment landscape, complete with hover-dodgems, disposable hot air balloons, bouncy floors, and escape towers.

It is interesting to observe the emphasis placed on technology in this scheme – and in the work of Archigram – which can be seen as a response to the advances that were taking place during the 1960s, such as the Apollo space programme, Sea-Lab, the introduction of the hovercraft and the Boeing 707. Whilst many of these technological developments were a direct result of cold war research programmes, they were all perceived to extend the capabilities of mankind, and as a result technology was seen as a form of social emancipation which was to be embraced. Rock music itself depended upon new technology, not just for the amplification of instruments and the emergence of the electric guitar, but

also for the advent of television which played a significant role in its rapid rise in popularity.

Fisher's fascination with technology is manifest in his Automat project of 1968, which he carried out in collaboration with fellow student David Harrison. The liberal pedagogical stance assumed by the Architectural Association at this time meant that they were positively encouraged to develop their own approach to architectural design, and as a result the project emerged out of a sustained period of practical experimentation. Automat was an attempt to create a self-articulating form which altered shape in response to its users' changing physical requirements. In order to achieve this they created a rudimentary low-pressure pneumatic structure which was articulated using a system of internal bracing cables connected to high-pressure jacks which could selectively expand or contract the structure at a ratio of 80:1. Although some problems were encountered with fabrication, the structure was exhibited at the Paris Biennale in 1969, and the project was featured in Peter Cook's publication *Experimental Architecture* in 1970.

Of all of the new technologies emerging during the 1960s, it was pneumatic structures that most appeared to capture the imagination of a new generation of architects. Architectural critic Reyner Banham observed in an article entitled 'Monumental

Of all the new technologies emerging during the 1960s, it was pneumatic structures that most appeared to capture the imagination of a new generation of architects. The culture of inflatability had a vitality and sense of fun generally missing in modern architecture.

Windbags', which appeared in *New Society* during April 1968, that in architectural circles, 'What is new is the confluence between changing taste and advances in plastic technology. The taste that has been turned off by the rectangular format of the official modern architecture ... is turned right on by the apparent do-it-yourself potential of low pressure inflatable technology.'

Banham's comments were used as a preface to an issue of *Architectural Design* magazine entitled 'Pneu World' which was published later in the same year. This became an influential document in the late 1960s, as it was the first major survey of pneumatic structures, and was guest edited by Fisher's collaborator on Automat, David Harrison, together with fellow AA students Johnny Devas, Mike Davies, David Martin and Simon Conolly. The individual projects, which were drawn from a wide range of sources, were considered not only in terms of their different constructional typologies, but also for the way in which they were capable of redefining the traditional relationship between people and their environment. Coincidentally, the same magazine carried a small news item announcing the death of modernist architectural historian Siegfried Gideon, who had been a powerful advocate of the kinds of architecture these new technologies sought to replace.

Although Banham's comments on inflatable structures indicate some of the reasons why pneumatic structures became so popular within a relatively short space of time, it was not only their new shapes and forms that appealed to designers: a number of other inherent characteristics reinforced their appropriateness. Firstly, there was the matter of their environmental responsiveness and ephemerality, which stood in stark contrast to the increasingly monumental and static forms of modernity. Secondly, the cheapness and simplicity of these structures meant that they could be created or owned by anyone, a 'democratic' approach to spatial enclosure that was very much attuned to the times, and thirdly, their disposability connected with a pre-environmentally aware consumer consciousness, that still believed in the notion of unlimited natural resources. Finally, there was the fact that 'ordinary' people could interact with these structures; the culture of inflatability had a vitality and sense of fun that was missing in the formal properties of much modern architecture. As Peter Cook observed in *Experimental Architecture*, in comparison to other architectural forms, 'Pneumatics have been far more popular with the general public: a condition which is rare in anything experimental.'

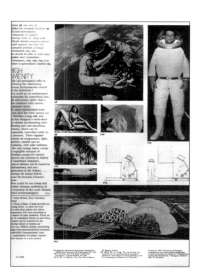

Dynamat

Whilst studying for his Diploma at the AA (1969–71) under Peter Cook, Fisher continued to investigate the potential of inflatable technology, and took a particular interest in the way it could create environments able to respond quickly to a user's changing physical requirements. This idea was explored in Dynamat, a project carried out with fellow student and co-editor of 'Pneu World', Simon Conolly.

The Dynamat project was essentially an extension work on Automat, but resolved many of its fabrication problems and increased the range of its potential application. Fisher and Conolly constructed a full-sized prototype panel of Dynamat which was exhibited in 1971 at 'Deubau', the German International Building Exhibition in Essen. The structure consisted of a series of inflatable cells combined in groups, which could be selectively expanded or contracted to produce changes in form. Whereas these movements had been controlled by pneumatic jacks on Automat, a simpler system was designed for Dynamat in which air routes between adjacent cells were controlled by a series of valves which opened and closed in pre-programmed sequences.

In its deflated state, Dynamat could be stored in the boot of a car for easy transportation, and individual panels could be combined to create a continuous surface which was shaped to enclose space, and to provide shelter for people or objects. An advanced control system was developed for the project which allowed for the sequential programming of the structure. Different configurations were stored on pre-recorded cassettes and presented the user with a range of possible spatial environments, or more complex sequences of enclosure which responded to, for instance, environmental changes in the diurnal cycle. As the programming of Dynamat increased in sophistication, it became obvious that the real usefulness of these structures lay in applications where performance criteria were more demanding than for traditional forms of architecture, where purpose-built temporary mobile structures would be more appropriate than more fixed and permanent solutions.

In addition to its appearance at 'Deubau', Dynamat was featured in an article entitled 'Pneu Moves' published in 1972 in *Architectural Design*. Fisher also presented a paper on the research at the Delft 'Pneumatic Structures Symposium' in September of the same year. However, whilst the technical aspects of the project received widespread interest, Fisher and Conolly were also fascinated by the social implications of such new technologies. Fisher explored this through a series of drawings which showed how the Dynamat structure could be deployed within the lives of 'ordinary' people. These cartoon images related 'The Adventures of 'Amersham 'Arry', a stereotypical, suburban London character, who was depicted in various scenarios with his inflatable Dynamat which could be reconfigured via his 'ever attentive "dial-a-style" modem'. In this respect, Fisher's work began to reflect more of the low-key approach to technology assumed by David Greene in his Bottery project of 1969, which was more engaged with the idea of everyday life than the spectacular environments proposed by Peter Cook and Ron Herron.

> Amersham 'Arry was a stereotypical character from suburban London who was depicted in various scenarios with his inflatable Dynamat, which could be reconfigured via his 'ever attentive "dial-a-style" modem'.

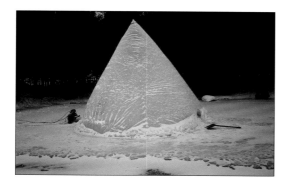

Besides the content of the drawings, the cartoon form used for the Amersham 'Arry drawings was also interesting in a number of ways. Having entered the avant-garde repertoire through Pop Art and in particular the work of Roy Lichtenstein, this style had been adopted by several members of Archigram in the early 1960s, and used to depict their schemes in the manner of contemporary science fiction publications, which themselves were engaged in foretelling future environments. Besides its popular appeal and cultural connotations, the cartoon form allowed for the representation of time sequences, and enabled Fisher to communicate the dynamic qualities of his work. In this way, these cartoonified representations were a form of escape from 'rapidograph modernity', the precise ink-on-tracing drawings that portrayed architecture as a static object to be revered, rather than an active event which demanded a more lively form of depiction.

Besides Dynamat, Fisher's interest in the everyday deployment of advanced technologies also influenced his Project for the Luxury Conversion of an Austin A40, which was carried out in the summer of 1971. This design can be seen as the antithesis of Ron Herron's legendary Walking City of 1964, which consisted of a series of unwieldy, mechanically mobilised, architectural structures, depicted striding past Manhattan Island. Herron's powerful image was seen as important because it performed a critique of urbanism, suggesting by implication that despite its skyscrapers, New York, as a permanent nucleated city, constituted an outdated approach to human habitation. Fisher's approach to nomadic existence was less monumental and concerned the adaptation of a family car into a specialised vehicle for 'touring', a suburban leisure pursuit that had gained popularity

During the 1970s Fisher was interested in creating disposable architectural products for the consumer market. He began by marketing the Plastic Pillow Pack under the aegis of Air Structures Design (ASD) which he set up with fellow student Simon Conolly whilst at the Architectural Association. This was followed later in the decade by Iceloo, a spray-up play structure created for the Canadian market in collaboration with Jon Hardy.

THE RESPONSIVE DWELLING BLURRED THE DISTINCTION BETWEEN THE BUILDING AND THE ORGANIC WORLD OF THE INHABITANT

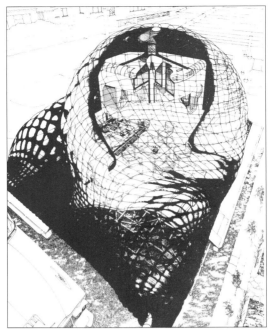 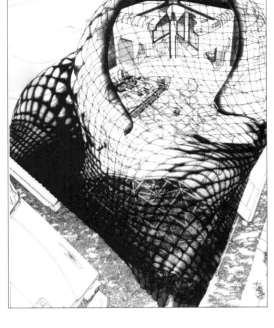

during the 1960s. Whereas Amersham 'Arry had been able to call on the services of the high-tech Dynamat, the owners of the Austin A40 were supplied with their very own inflatable village, Burton Constable, which was transported in the boot and could be deployed wherever the car was parked to create a rural ambience.

The design for the Austin A40 project, like the Adult Theme Park of 1970, was commissioned by Margaret Duckett, who was the design director of the *Weekend Telegraph Magazine*, which frequently ran articles on innovative architectural ideas. Both these schemes were carried out by Air Structures Design (ASD), a company set up by Fisher and Conolly during the last two years of their training at the Architectural Association. The purpose of ASD was twofold. Firstly, very few institutions were actively involved with research into the new light-weight technologies, so Fisher and Conolly decided that the best way of learning about them was by carrying out live projects, such as the construction of a lightweight structure for the Bishop of Bath and Wells. Secondly, ASD provided them with a means of generating funds that allowed them to finance their own research and development, including the construction of the Dynamat prototypes. Thus ASD designed and marketed the Plastic Pillow Pack, a simple do-it-yourself, 20 foot by 12 inch low pressure inflatable structure that was advertised for sale in several architectural magazines.

Whilst Fisher acknowledges the significant influence that Archigram had on his work as a student and his subsequent career as a designer of performance

environments, in some ways the establishment of ASD constituted a significant point of departure from Archigram's approach. Fisher's technical curiosity and his interest in the physical realisation of ideas meant that he was unwilling to operate within the confines of 'paper architecture', a condition that characterised the majority of Archigram's creative output, and that of his fellow students.

Fisher's attempt to distance himself from this approach can be seen in his own teaching at the AA where he ran a design studio from 1973 to 1976 after finishing his own studies. The name of the studio, the Nice Ideas Unit, was an ironic comment on the lack of interest in the practical realisation of projects within the school at this time. The unit was strongly biased towards hands-on experimentation, and carried out a series of live projects in collaboration with local people. This was not simply a pragmatic stance, as Fisher set the students briefs for which no precedent existed, forcing them into formal and technical innovation that resulted in structures such as the climbing net system and a 'superslide' designed for children in Islington.

Throughout this period Fisher continued to develop the ideas of Dynamat, which eventually gave rise to his Responsive Dwelling Project of 1973–75, in which the structure of the environment became more akin to a living system and 'the division between the technics of the building and the organic world of the inhabitant become blurred'. This led to one final piece of work in this area of speculation, which proposed an aquatic habitat that was completely 'constructed' out of genetically modified natural plant matter. This constituted the ultimate manifestation of architecture as a 'living system'. This project was exhibited at ArtNet in 1974.

The otherworldliness of this final theoretical proposal was matched in a more practical sense by Fisher's work on the science-fiction film *Zardoz*, directed by John Boorman and shot in Southern Ireland during 1971. Fisher worked on the project with fellow AA graduate Piers Gough, who had been commissioned to design and construct a series of sets around an existing nineteenth-century building. The film, which starred Sean Connery, presented a vision of the future in which people had become manipulated by an invisible force, a familiar theme at the time due to the cold war. The sets consisted of a series of inflatable towers, and other retro-fitted pneumatic structures, which gave the environment its eerie quality. Driven by his self-confessed enthusiasm for pyrotechnics, Fisher managed to persuade the director and film crew to end the shoot by blowing up the set, which prefigured the kind of approach he has used since in the design of rock performances.

The *Zardoz* sets constitute an important moment in Fisher's career, in that his work appeared poised between two very different worlds: although the structures he created for the film were 'inhabitable', it was only in an imaginary sense rather than as part of everyday lived reality. As a consequence, these structures took on a representational quality that was not present in Dynamat and mark the point at which his work became involved in a more 'staged' audience/performer relationship.

The Responsive Dwelling Project attempted to bring together structural, cybernetic and environmental systems into a single matrix which Fisher eventually realised was a mechanical analogue for what should have been a bio-technical system. This was addressed in a later project which proposed an aquatic habitat created out of genetically modified natural plant matter.

Despite the 'Pneu World' optimism of the late 1960s, the technologically responsive environments proposed by Fisher and his colleagues did not emerge into mainstream architectural practice during the 1970s, nor did they make any meaningful impact on the built environment. Rather, architecture remained on the whole an internalised discourse primarily concerned with form and lacking any engagement with wider social or cultural concerns. Throughout his student training and in his early career, Fisher had demonstrated that his interest lay beyond this narrow outlook and that in spite of the advanced technological nature of his work, at its heart lay a concern with the experiences of ordinary people, and their engagement with, and enjoyment of, dynamic or event-based structures.

His involvement in the staging of rock concerts began in 1977, when he was approached by Andrew Sanders to create a series of inflatables for Pink Floyd's 'Animals' world tour. The loose conceptual framework of the accompanying album dealt with a number of issues that preoccupied the band's youthful audience, including the banalisation of everyday life under the forces of capitalism, and the oppressive nature of institutionalised authority.

Fisher's and Sander's role in the project concerned a visualisation of these issues, transforming them from intellectual concepts into a series of powerful icons or cultural signifiers that could be used by Pink Floyd in a way that not only entertained the audience, but also helped to reinforce the message being carried in the music. To this end, inspired by the ideas of Roger Waters, he created a series of characters that represented a stereotypical 'nuclear' family, including a businessman in a pinstriped suit, his 'blousy' wife on a sofa, and their somewhat obese son and daughter. The daughter held on to the hand of a third child, but only half a child, which was a humorous reference to the fact that in official statistics, the 'average' family produced 2.5 children.

The inflatable family was moored above the stage and accompanied by the trappings of its consumer lifestyle including a television set, refrigerator and a large pink Cadillac. The size of the individual inflatables was the subject of much discussion between Fisher and the band: Roger Waters wanted them to be life-size, but Fisher believed that they should be much larger. This conviction demonstrates Fisher's immediate grasp of the main issue at stake in the 'staging' of rock performances, namely that communication between the band and audience depends on the scale of the event. It was eventually agreed that the figures would be three times life-size, but in later commissions for Pink Floyd and other clients Fisher enlarged them even further.

For the 'Animals' performance Fisher created a series of characters that represented a stereotypical 'nuclear' family, including a businessman in a pinstriped suit, his 'blousy wife', and their two and a half obese children, all of whom floated in the air alongside a range of consumer goods.

In addition to the 'nuclear family', Fisher's commission also entailed the mass production of a number of large pigs, which served to represent authority, and in particular the police, in a simple and direct symbolic form. The original inflatable pig, which was used as a part of the powerful 'Animals' album cover was created by Jeffrey Shaw of the Amsterdam-based Eventstructure Research Group. In the live shows, an inflatable pig appeared at the rear of the stadium during the relevant song, and flew over the heads of the audience snorting, until it disappeared behind the stage. A few seconds later, a disposable, helium-filled pig floated up into the night sky above the stage and exploded, much to the delight of the audience.

This 'staged' display of Water's anti-authoritarian sentiments, which attacked the organisational basis of society, served as a powerful means of identification between the band and their audience, and yet it is interesting to note that this occurred at a time when Pink Floyd was enjoying huge commercial success. This illustrates the paradox that lies at the heart of all rock performance which operates as both a form of social resistance and also as a commodified spectacle.

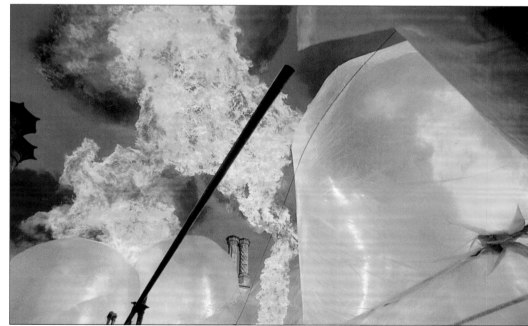

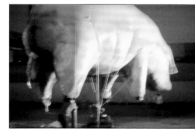

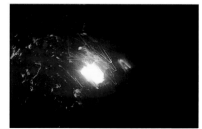

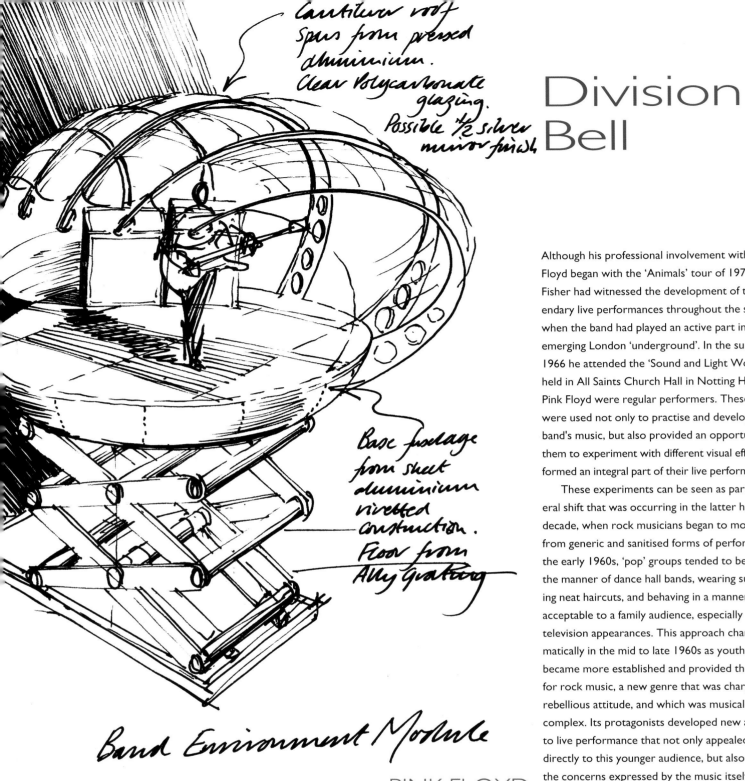

Cantilever roof
spars from pressed
aluminium.
Clear Polycarbonate
glazing.
Possible ½ silver
mirror finish.

Base fuselage
from sheet
aluminium
rivetted
construction.
Floor from
Alloy Grating

Band Environment Module

Division Bell

Although his professional involvement with Pink Floyd began with the 'Animals' tour of 1977, Mark Fisher had witnessed the development of their legendary live performances throughout the sixties, when the band had played an active part in the emerging London 'underground'. In the summer of 1966 he attended the 'Sound and Light Workshops' held in All Saints Church Hall in Notting Hill, where Pink Floyd were regular performers. These sessions were used not only to practise and develop the band's music, but also provided an opportunity for them to experiment with different visual effects which formed an integral part of their live performances.

These experiments can be seen as part of a general shift that was occurring in the latter half of the decade, when rock musicians began to move away from generic and sanitised forms of performance. In the early 1960s, 'pop' groups tended to be styled in the manner of dance hall bands, wearing suits, sporting neat haircuts, and behaving in a manner deemed acceptable to a family audience, especially during television appearances. This approach changed dramatically in the mid to late 1960s as youth cultures became more established and provided the impetus for rock music, a new genre that was charged with a rebellious attitude, and which was musically more complex. Its protagonists developed new approaches to live performance that not only appealed more directly to this younger audience, but also reflected the concerns expressed by the music itself. In the case of bands such as The Rolling Stones or The Who, the excitement of their live performances was as much dependent on the energy and charisma of their individual members as it was on the musical virtuosity of the band, with songs of youthful rebellion

PINK FLOYD
DEMONSTRATE A MORE
CEREBRAL OR ART-BASED
APPROACH TO ROCK
PERFORMANCE

underscored by the frenzied movements and pouting insolence of Mick Jagger, or the destructive antics of Pete Townsend and Roger Daltrey.

Whilst these groups tended to connect with their audience through an aggressive expression of disaffected sentiments, with performances of songs such as '(I can't get no) Satisfaction' or 'Won't get fooled again', the music ethos and live approach of a group such as Pink Floyd during the same period was altogether different. During their early years in particular, Pink Floyd appeared much more concerned with constructing an alternative reality for their audience than with 'kicking against the establishment'. Shows staged by Pink Floyd during the late 1960s represented a more psychedelic, cerebral or art-based approach to rock music when compared to the visceral performances of The Rolling Stones. They would typically consist of a series of lengthy, atmospheric and predominantly instrumental pieces of music with titles such as 'Interstellar Overdrive' or 'Astronomy Domine', which alluded to mysterious other-worldly dimensions. Rather than the performers themselves serving as a visual focus for the audience, their soundscapes were complemented by visual effects created through the use of moving oil wheels, coloured lights, and projections of films and ether-injected slides. These transformed the performance space, and placed the audience within a 'total experience' of sound and light.

The atmosphere generated by these visual effects was similarly invoked by the powerful artwork created for the album covers, which dispensed with the ubiquitous group photograph and replaced it with imagery that attempted to convey the quality and mood of Pink Floyd's music. The majority of this work was created by Storm Thorgerson and Aubrey Powell at the highly influential graphic design practice Hipgnosis. In his recent book *Mind over Matter*, which catalogues his work for the band, Thorgerson writes that: 'In conversation with the Floyd it seemed that the best way to "represent" the music visually was to

In their early live shows Pink Floyd were concerned with constructing an alternative reality for their audience, creating atmospheric soundscapes that were complemented by the psychedelic visual effects of moving oil wheels, coloured lights, and projections of film and ether-injected slides.

show some of the things that they were interested in and to present them in a manner resonant with the music. Marvel comics, astrology, alchemy, swirling patterns, outer space and infra red weird photography were thrown together like an immiscible oil and water bubble at an early Floyd gig, superimposed upon each other, drifting around in a dreamlike fashion, not a million miles away from certain minor hallucinatory states that are alleged to result from taking narcotic substances.'

These comments raise the issue of drug use in the 1960s, and its effects on rock music which became more pronounced in the latter half of the decade, after LSD became available in 1965. The sudden dramatic increase in the recreational use of drugs may also be attributable to the steady erosion of optimism experienced during the sixties, which occurred as a direct result of a series of events and crises that affected young peoples' lives and outlook, including the ongoing cold war, civil rights disturbances, the assassinations of President Kennedy and Martin Luther King, nuclear weapons tests, and the Vietnam war.

The response of youth to such events appeared to range between two extremes: either radical political activism, as evidenced by the student riots in Paris in May 1968, or a drug-induced escapism. The compromise solution was offered by the hippie generation, who reached their apotheosis in the 'Summer of Love' of 1967, rejecting authority and positing an

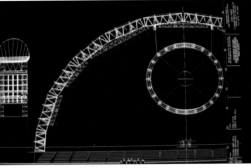
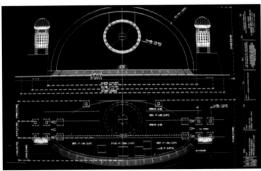
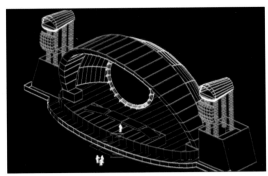

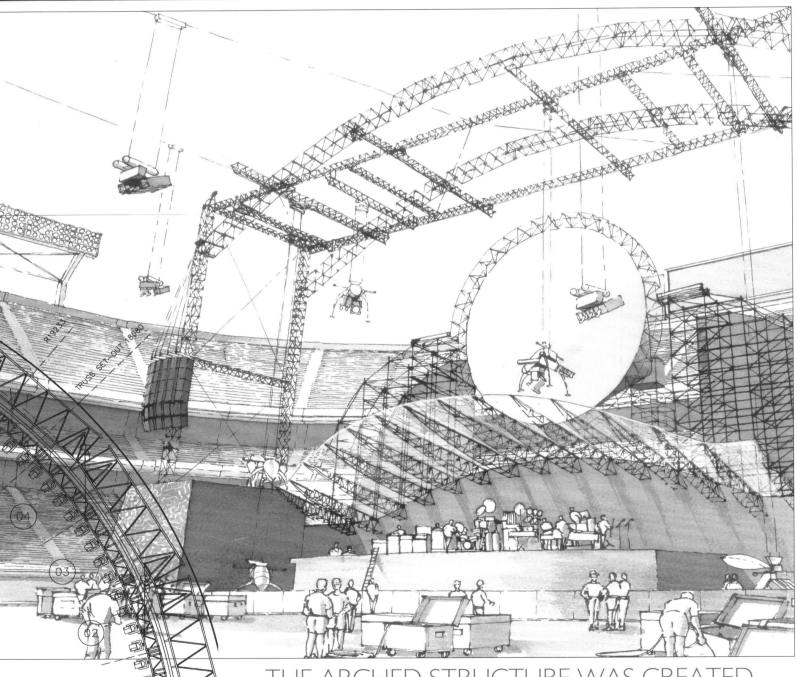

THE ARCHED STRUCTURE WAS CREATED
OUT OF A STANDARD SYSTEM OF TRUSSES
THAT WERE ADAPTED BY USING SPECIALLY
MANUFACTURED SPACING PIECES

alternative lifestyle that was based on a respect for the environment, free love, unregulated drug-use, beat literature and groovy psychedelic music.

In many ways, the origins of Pink Floyd's approach to live performance lie within this moment, with the psychedelic nature of their shows attempting to capture (or perhaps enhance) the same intensity of experience as that induced by drugs: a heightened sense of perception or form of reverie in which individuals were not confronted with the inadequacies of their everyday life, but transported beyond them into another realm. As such, these performance environments were places in which audiences could 'lose' themselves, not through the externalisation of aggression, but by attaining an internalised trance-like state.

In 1994 Fisher began working on the 'Division Bell' show for Pink Floyd alongside production designer Marc Brickman. This tour was only the second undertaken by Pink Floyd since the departure of one of the original members of the band, Roger Waters, in the early 1980s. Moving away from their early emphasis on reverie, in the final live shows carried out with Waters the underlying message had become more political in intent, and the band had developed more of a narrative approach, culminating in the spectacular 'Wall' performance of 1980, which used highly specific visuals that related directly to the lyrics of individual songs.

After the departure of Waters, David Gilmour assumed responsibility for the form and content of Pink Floyd's live performances and the 'Division Bell' show sought to recapture something of the original sixties spirit of the band. The project itself underwent several stages in its conception, starting with a series of ideas produced by Marc Brickman, who had been responsible for the show which accompanied the 'Momentary Lapse of Reason' album in 1987.

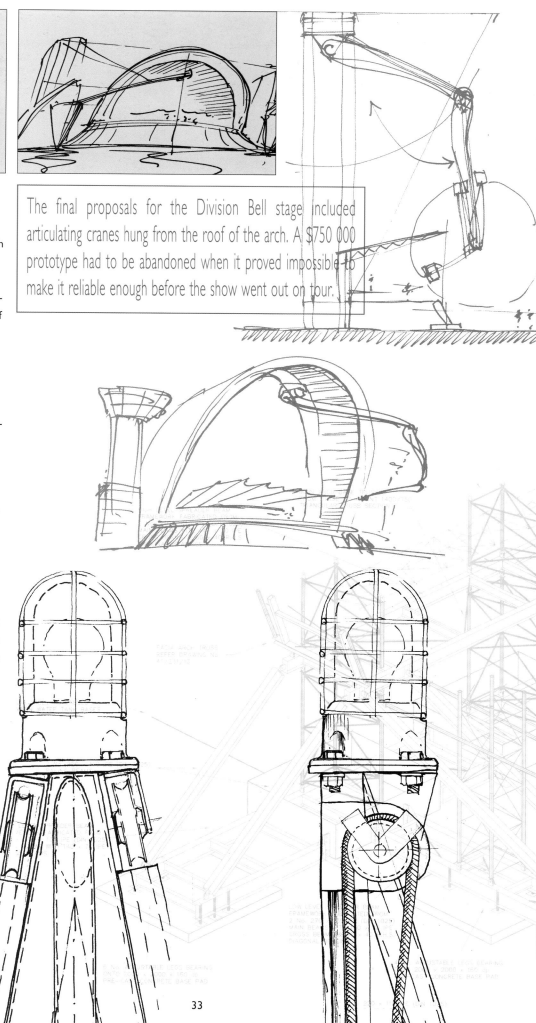

The final proposals for the Division Bell stage included articulating cranes hung from the roof of the arch. A $750 000 prototype had to be abandoned when it proved impossible to make it reliable enough before the show went out on tour.

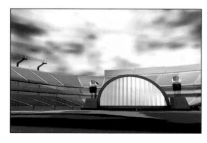

A number of standardised structural systems have been developed which pack efficiently into vehicles for touring. For the Division Bell show, the trusses for the main arch slid inside one another and were dimensioned to fit exactly across the width of a truck. Also the curved structure for the lighting was designed as an 'L' shape and had its third plane of bracing added during assembly.

THE STAGE WAS CREATED OUT OF A TRANSPARENT MODULAR DECKING SYSTEM WHICH ALLOWED LIGHTING FROM BELOW

Fisher's response to the 'Division Bell' was to conceive the stadium as a dream landscape inhabited by the audience. In comparison to his contemporaneous work for the Rolling Stones (such as 'Voodoo Lounge'), his initial proposals for the show were dominated by a waterfall which provided the backdrop to the stage, and a series of pod-like structures or 'environment modules' constructed out of aluminium and polycarbonate, which were mounted on individual scissor lifts. Marc Brickman's ideas included a gigantic arched structure, which had a powerful physical presence that Fisher was asked to develop into a practical and tourable design.

Working with Neil Thomas from the engineering firm Atelier One, Fisher realised Brickman's initial idea as a 40-metre wide semi-circular arch, which took into account the need to scale the form to the size of a sports stadium and the logistics of building it within a limited amount of time. The main structure was created out of a standard system of rectangular trusses which were rented to save on capital costs, and adapted by the use of specially made spacer pieces to create the unique shape required for the show.

This was the first time that Fisher had worked with a generic system and reconfigured it to create what appeared to be a bespoke design solution. It was also a complete contradiction of the approach to ephemeral structures he had taken during his training at the Architectural Association. This had involved the design of high-tech, specially manufactured systems of components, which could then be combined in various forms to allow for multiple uses and spontaneity.

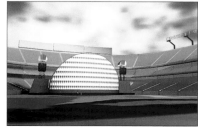

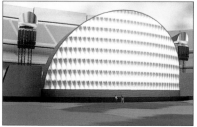

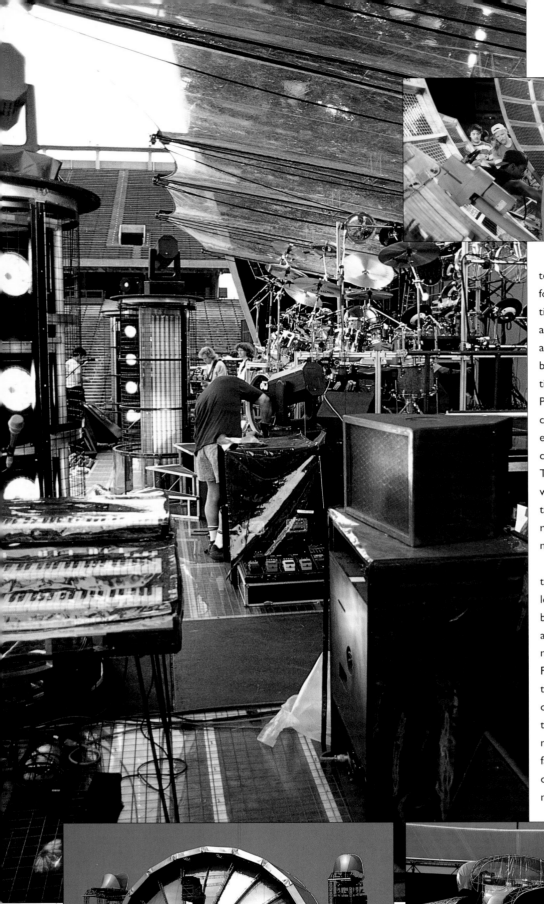

Since 1994, Fisher has often used this *ad hoc* technique in his stage designs, adapting the generic forms of low-tech components into new configurations. In the 'Division Bell' show, the simplicity of this approach meant that it was possible to build the main arch in seven hours, with each triangulated section being hinged to its neighbour and swung into position. The framework was covered in a reinforced PVC membrane; the rear wall of the stage was curved in profile into a cyclorama to heighten lighting effects, and was supported by a pneumatic structure consisting of a series of high pressure radial tubes. This strategy drew on Fisher's previous experience with more architectural uses of inflatable technology, taking advantage of the fact that it could be erected rapidly, but accepting the inherently vulnerable nature of its construction.

The huge size and profile of the completed structure meant that it was susceptible to effects of wind loadings, and in order to overcome this a water-filled base was devised by Fisher and Thomas which anchored the whole arch to the ground, and also made it possible to level the structure on any site. For further stability, the arched form was fixed to the two huge sentinel-like PA towers located either side of the stage. In addition to providing the housing for the sound system, these structures were each surmounted by a hooded enclosure from which the infamous pig inflatables, that have become a trademark of Pink Floyd's live shows, sprang at the appropriate moment.

The need to scale the arch to proportions that were appropriate for its use in sports stadia meant that it could not function easily as a shelter for the performers and their equipment. Fisher addressed this issue as he had in previous shows by creating a second, lower-level structure with a transparent roof, which left the rear wall free for lighting effects and image projection. The fixtures used to create these effects were not only located above and to the sides of the stage, attached to the rim of the arch structure, but also beneath the stage. This was created out of a complex transparent modular decking system, which had to be weatherproof to protect the lower-level technical deck, where the lights and other equipment were located. The front of the stage was made out of an apron of sloping periactoi units. These special modules consisted of a series of rotating prisms with a different finish applied to each of their three facets. In their least dynamic state, the units were programmed to place a matte black surface uppermost, providing a strong border to the edge of the stage. The other faces of the prisms could be rotated to reveal either banks of lights which were programmed into sequences, or a mirrored surface which reflected light from other sources.

During the show, these and other effects were controlled from the lighting desk located in the centre of the stadium. A second structure was created which protected the control desks and projection platform from the elements, whilst also providing seating for VIPs. This took on an insect-like form, a carapace protecting the vulnerable hi-tech equipment, and was clad in the same silver material as the main arch, but with a series of stepped roof forms that were retracted in good weather.

THE VISUAL EFFECTS WERE CONTROLLED
FROM AN INSECT-LIKE STRUCTURE LOCATED
IN THE CENTRE OF THE AUDITORIUM

It is interesting to compare the main arched 'Division Bell' structure with an earlier design for the band that had been partially built by Fisher and his former partner Jonathan Park, for Britannia Row, the production company owned by Pink Floyd. Following their 'Animals' tour in 1977, the band had decided to pursue an earlier idea that they had had for a stage in the form of a pyramid, and Fisher and Park were commissioned to build a 20-metre high version created from lightweight lattice girders and featuring a helium-filled detachable upper section that was designed to float away above the stage. The project was eventually shelved, but the drawings provide a powerful impression of what it might have been like to experience, and how radically different this would have been to the arch form. For whilst the pyramid presented a symbolic object for contemplation, the arched structure in the 'Division Bell' show had the effect of creating a tunnel or gateway into another world, in which events related to the music could be enacted.

The spectacular lighting sequences which brought this huge form to life, and dissolved its physicality, were created by Marc Brickman, and were integrated with a series of other special effects, several of which were designed in collaboration with Fisher. The lighting designs utilised Varilight technology, a hi-tech system developed for Genesis in the early 1980s, in which individual units could be computer controlled to change not only the colour of a beam, but also its intensity, direction and the pattern it threw on a surface. These highly versatile modules were programmed into a series of complex sequences, and further enhanced by the use of projections and laser beams.

THE ARCHED STRUCTURE CREATED A GATEWAY INTO ANOTHER WORLD WHERE EVENTS RELATED TO THE MUSIC HAPPENED

The lasers used in the 1994 performances were a type of copper vapour, used in heavy industry for cutting steel, and differed from traditional lasers by having a wider beam and being orange rather than green in colour. In keeping with this quest for innovation, a liquid light projection system was employed in the 'Division Bell' show which had never been seen on this scale before. When taken together, the kaleidoscopic lighting sequences and the projections of immiscible oil and water patterns created the kinds of psychedelic effects that had, in less spectacular form, accompanied earlier Pink Floyd performances. These were further enhanced by the use of special mechanical strobe lights which had originally been invented in the 1960s for Pink Floyd by Peter Wynne Wilson and David Gilmour and were recreated in a more powerful form for the 1994 tour.

In addition to the effects created from the front of stage, one of the major ingredients of the 'Division Bell' show was the use of film, which was back projected on to a large circular screen which hovered above the stage. This powerful circular form had been a fixture in Pink Floyd's live performances since the early 1970s, and had become emblematic of the band, hovering above the stage like a huge eye in the sky. However, rather than treat it as a static element that was present from the start of the performance, Fisher designed the screen so that it could be stored flat on the floor at the rear of the stage and winched into position during the performance, revealing itself to the audience.

During the late 1960s and early 1970s, Pink Floyd produced several soundtrack albums, with their moody atmospheric music providing the perfect backdrop to cult films such as *More* (1969) whose plot centred around the use of recreational drug use,

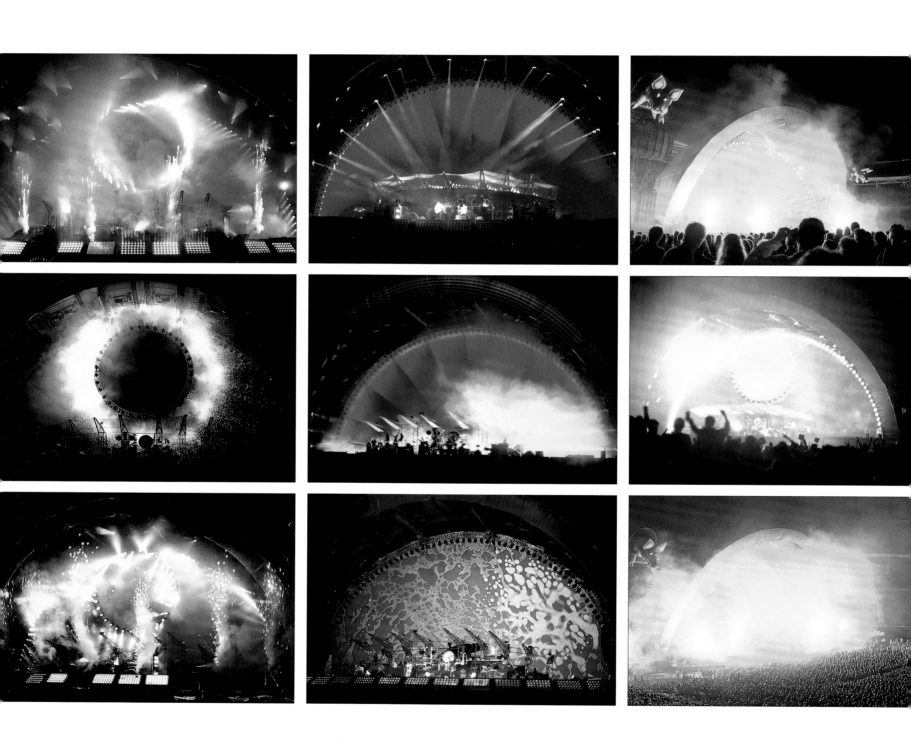

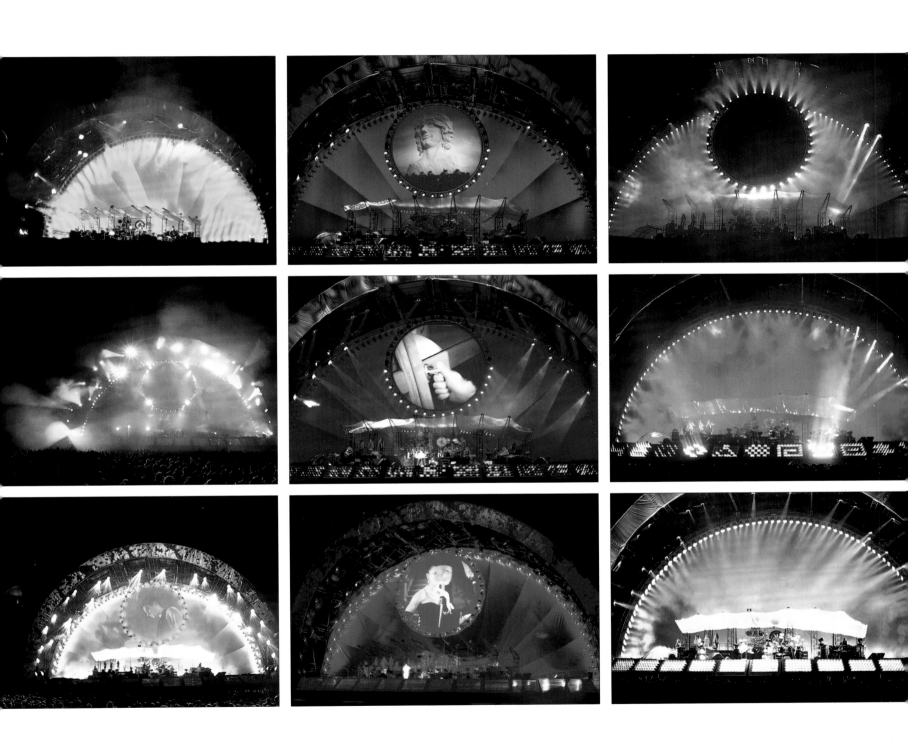

THE FINALE OF THE SHOW FEATURED A HUGE MIRROR BALL WHICH ROSE OUT OF THE REAR OF THE MIXING DESK STRUCTURE BEFORE BREAKING OPEN AND FLOODING THE STADIUM WITH LIGHT

Zabriskie Point (1970) which concerned the trials and tribulations of youth subculture, and the baffling *La Valle* or *The Valley Obscured by Clouds* of 1972. Given their involvement in these films, it is not surprising that the band chose to use film as an appropriate visual means to accompany their own live performances. As a medium, film differs considerably from video, which has now become an almost ubiquitous element in contemporary rock productions. Whereas video lends itself more towards a raw documentary approach, for the audience, cinematography carries connotations of a higher art form, and has a much greater resolution, particularly when shot using the high-quality 70mm film favoured by Pink Floyd.

For the 'Division Bell' show, the band commissioned Storm Thorgerson to create several new films, and to update some footage that had been used on previous tours. The return of Thorgerson in the role of art director, both for the films and also the album artwork, was symbolic of the band's attempt to recapture the spirit of Pink Floyd during its creative peak in the mid-1970s.

In the early eighties the creative agenda of the band changed, and they started to use the more fiercely satirical cartoon forms of Gerald Scarfe for visual effect rather than the often surreal images of Thorgerson. These reappeared in the 'Division Bell' show in the films made to accompany the title track from the album, and the song 'High Hopes'. The latter

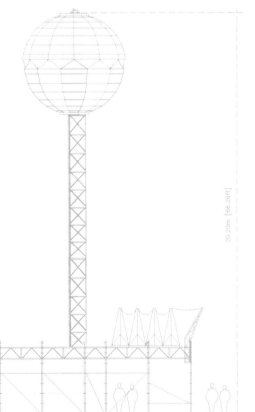

concerned memories of childhood and Thorgerson utilised oversized objects to represent the fact that children perceive the scale of things in relation to themselves, seeing them as taller and larger than they actually are. Several of the other films draw on the same surrealistic imagery, using Dali-esque melting clocks, and the same kinds of enigmatic relationships between objects found in the work of the artist René Magritte.

This visual language, which also underpinned the images created for the album artwork, connects with the music of Pink Floyd because of its suggestion of an alternative reality. Surrealism, which literally meant 'above' or 'beyond' reality, sought to create a connection between dreaming and waking states, a condition that the band's live shows tend to invoke in the observer.

Thorgerson's refurbishment of footage that accompanied older songs such as 'Money' was carried out as a result of Gilmour's preferred approach to the 'Division Bell' show, which stood in stark contrast to that used for 'The Wall'. Whereas the latter show had been concerned with performing material from a single album, with a strong narrative, for 'Division Bell', Gilmour chose instead to include material drawn from the entire œuvre of the band, with each song considered as a separate entity rather than contributing to an overall message.

This anthological approach went further than Gilmour's choice of music and the re-use of old film. Fisher was asked to recreate a number of memorable 'gags' from previous performances including the appearance of the Pigs from the 'Animals' tour, which glowered at the audience menacingly from their position above the PA towers, and the crashing airplane sequence, that had been first performed for 'The Wall'. For the grand finale, however, Fisher was charged with creating a spectacular new effect: a huge mirror ball which provided 'a focus for mystic veneration by drug-crazed fans'. This 6-metre diameter spherical feature packed down flat into the mixing desk structure, and rose to a height of 18 metres by means of a Tomcat Starlift retractable tower. As it reached its full extension the mirrorball cracked open and burst apart, flooding the stadium with light, before a final cataclysmic burst of fireworks ended the show.

In these final moments, the attention of the audience was drawn away from the stage and towards the patterns projected on to the stadium and into the night sky, while the band played on, providing the soundtrack for this mesmerising experience.

Urban Events

The Wall

Like television, newspapers and the cinema, rock music is essentially a metropolitan form of popular culture, having developed to meet the consumer demands of a mass audience. With its insistent rhythms and driving beat, rock appears to underscore the frantic pace of urban life, and through a host of technologies including jukeboxes, transistor radios, car stereos, 'boom boxes', 'ghetto blasters' and the Walkman, permeates the space of the city, and provides the soundtrack for the metropolitan experience.

Urban form figures in Fisher's stage designs in two distinct ways. The first concerns the relationship between the performance environment and the actual space of the city. The majority of rock concerts have little direct impact on the city, taking place either in smaller purpose-built venues located in downtown areas or in much larger sports stadia which are sited on the periphery due to their monumental scale. In both of these situations the rock event is essentially contained, which is to say that a clear differentiation exists between the performance environment and the space of the city. On a number of occasions, however, Fisher has been involved in blurring this distinction, creating performances that utilise the actual space and built form of the urban environment; effectively presenting the audience with the 'City as Event'. This approach is often used as a way of celebrating pivotal moments in a city's history, and provides a powerful symbolic marker for the multitudes that attend.

Fisher's second approach utilises urbanism at a representational level, employing architectural imagery as a connotative sign and creating environments that resonate with the audience at a symbolic or metaphorical level. These manifestations of the 'Event as City' often draw on contemporary cultural preoccupations for their themes and invoke alternative urban scenarios that are inhabited by the audience for the duration of the performance.

Both of these approaches can be seen in the two separate live projects associated with 'The Wall', a concept album released by Pink Floyd in 1979. This recording took as its theme the alienation of a rock star from his audience and drew upon architecture for its central metaphor. Working closely with Roger Waters, Fisher and his former partner Jonathan Park devised an accompanying performance in which a vast wall was gradually constructed on the stage, which represented the increasing sense of distance between the performer and audience. As Waters' fictional character Pink experienced the final phases of a mental breakdown, his sense of alienation was communicated through the architecture of the set, with the rockstar depicted all alone in a tiny hotel room juxtaposed against the colossal form of the completed wall.

During the second half of the performance, the band remained hidden from the audience behind the wall, which was used as a gigantic screen onto which were projected the savage animations of cartoonist Gerald Scarfe. The music itself served as a soundtrack to amplify this imagery, which was augmented by a series of malevolent inflatable figures created from Scarfe's cartoon drawings of the rock star's mother, wife and schoolteacher. Their ominous presence added to the overwhelming sense of paranoia induced by the performance, which was brought to a

THE WALL SERVED AS A METAPHOR FOR THE ALIENATION OF A ROCK STAR FROM HIS AUDIENCE

climax with the 'trial' of Pink, before the spectacular finale during which 'The Wall' was destroyed as a cathartic gesture.

'The Wall', which toured during 1980 and 1981, was by far the most ambitious show ever staged at that time, but was only seen by audiences in Los Angeles, Long Island, London and Dortmund, and only performed twenty-nine times. As a concept it received unfavourable criticism at the hands of some critics of the period who had been influenced by the punk rock movement of the late 1970s. Punk rock was, in part, a rebellion against the very 'high-art' approach to music epitomised by Pink Floyd, but interestingly 'The Wall' went on to reach a larger audience later in the eighties when it was turned into a film by Alan Parker, starring the 'new-wave' vocalist Bob Geldof as Pink.

City as event

In 1990 Fisher and Park designed a one-off outdoor production of 'The Wall' in Berlin. Waters (who had separated from Pink Floyd in the early eighties) planned the event as a response to the fall of the Berlin Wall in 1989, and Fisher Park were employed to design the show. The 10-metre high cardboard wall of the original show was replaced by a 25-metre high polystyrene and scaffolding structure 168 metres wide. It was scaled to suit the 10-hectare site on the derelict Potsdamer Platz, a part of the no man's land between East and West Germany that is regarded by Berliners as the symbolic heart of the former city. The stage itself was 30 metres across, and was designed to accommodate not only the band, which was assembled specially for the performance by Waters, but also an 80-piece orchestra, a 150-person

In the original show that toured during 1980 and 1981, 'The Wall' was performed by Pink Floyd in front of audiences of 15,000 people. The spectacular restaging of this event in Potsdamer Platz in Berlin during 1990 was attended by a crowd of over 250,000, and was presented by Roger Waters and other rock luminaries including Joni Mitchell, Brian Adams, Cyndi Lauper, Sinead O'Connor and Thomas Dolby.

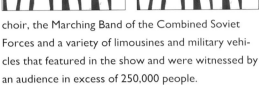

choir, the Marching Band of the Combined Soviet Forces and a variety of limousines and military vehicles that featured in the show and were witnessed by an audience in excess of 250,000 people.

Potsdamer Platz is currently being redeveloped as a dense commercial district in the reconstituted centre of a united Berlin, and its potential as a venue for performance was shortlived, but offered Fisher Park the opportunity to use the real space of a city and operate outside the usual confines of a stadium. Working on 'The Wall' in Berlin was not the first time that Fisher had been involved in the transformation of the real fabric of the city into an event. In 1986, Fisher Park were commissioned to design a show for Jean-Michel Jarre in the centre of Houston, Texas, as part of the celebrations marking the 150th anniversary of the city. This spectacular performance was carried out in front of an estimated audience of one million people, and the city formed a dramatic backdrop for the show, with its skyscrapers illuminated by lasers and used as surfaces upon which to project gigantic images. Similar performances were planned for New York and Tokyo but were not carried out, although Jarre performed two shows in London Docklands in 1988. Here he used the old warehouses around the edges of the docks, and projected images onto them which drew in part on the history of the area, overlaying the physical structures with images of the past.

Both 'The Wall' and Jean-Michel Jarre's shows were spectacular ephemeral events staged in the midst of historic change, and can be seen as indicators of a new era in which the city was increasingly altering its *raison d'être*. London Docklands was

THE 'CITY AS EVENT' USES METROPOLITAN SPACE AS A PERFORMANCE ENVIRONMENT

rapidly undergoing redevelopment as a new financial centre whilst Berlin was moving towards unification. Both were coming to terms with the urban consequences of a post-industrial economy and with an increasing emphasis on the urban centre as a source of leisure activities and entertainment. This trend is still continuing, and city centres all over the world are being recast as entertainment complexes. It could be argued that some urban design solutions which have been introduced into places such as London, New York, Tokyo, Osaka and Las Vegas owe more to rock sets than traditional urban forms. In effect, what appears to be taking place is the theatricalisation of the city, a process anticipated in the work of Archigram and especially in Mike Webb's 'Sin Centre'. Many rock concert lighting designers have become increasingly involved in the floodlighting of city-centre buildings.

AQUAMATRIX
TOOK AS ITS THEME THE
EVOLUTION OF THE
EARTH AND MAN'S
DESTRUCTION OF THE
ENVIRONMENT

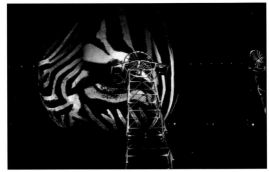

Besides his designs for rock concerts which consume the space of the city, Fisher's part in the theatricalisation of the city can also be seen in his work for the Lisbon Expo in 1998, a show entitled 'Aquamatrix', which was effectively a piece of urban entertainment. Like Jean-Michel Jarre's concert in London, this show was located in a former dock basin and took as its theme the evolution of the earth and man's destruction of the environment. Show director Alberto Lopes related the story to the audience through a series of images projected on to a 30-metre high egg-shaped inflatable, which was symbolically consumed towards the end of the performance.

Themes and narratives

The structuring of perfomance environments around visual themes is a design strategy Fisher has used frequently in his work for The Rolling Stones. This differs greatly from the approach used in his shows for Pink Floyd, which have tended to be either neutral architectures which act as a frame for the events taking place within them ('Division Bell'), or structured according to a distinctive linear narrative ('The Wall').

In his book *The Theming of America*, cultural theorist Mark Gottdiener examines the nature of thematically based environments, looking at a variety of restaurants, casinos, shopping malls and theme parks which embody this methodology. These are typically leisure experiences, and exemplify what Gottdiener refers to as 'large material forms which serve as containers for human interaction', a category into which rock shows may also be seen to fall. Gottdiener argues that the reason for the burgeoning use of theming as a strategy revolves around the development of consumerism generally, and he sees themed environments as a form of cultural production which seeks to use constructed space as a realm of symbols. Such environments function through a semiotic process and are organised around a set of symbolic motifs and sign objects which convey recognisable cultural meanings. People have been shown to derive enjoyment from thematic content: they find it stimulating and it generally helps them to differentiate otherwise similar products in the market place, whether they be restaurants, malls or rock and roll concerts.

Gottdiener also observes that whilst themed environments are designed to create a condition of empathy, in the wrong circumstances they can also fail to trigger a response in the user, producing what he calls 'a neutral relationship', whereby there has

been 'a failure of the symbolic content to stimulate'. There is also the possibility that theming can produce more negative responses or even displeasure. Fisher is aware of the potential dangers of alienating an audience, and generally chooses themes which have a contemporary relevance or which resonate with people's collective memories, allowing them to become emotionally involved with the performance. These are often developed by collaging together a

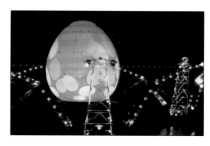

series of images, forms and motifs drawn from a wide range of popular sources, which are consciously chosen for their cultural significance. This creates an aura for the performance rather than a single overriding visual theme, presenting the audience with an open framework for interpretation and an opportunity for active consumption.

In many ways Fisher's approach recalls the 'Narrative Architecture' of Nigel Coates, who trained at the Architectural Association shortly after Fisher, and developed his design approach in collaboration with the NATO (Narrative Architecture Today) group of designers. Coates' methodology can be seen as a reaction against the Modernist preoccupation with design as an expression of integrity and honesty, and has the same disregard for the essentially reductivist 'form follows function' ideology as Fisher. In his essay entitled 'Streetstyle', published in 1988, Coates suggests that 'The purpose of architecture [is] open to redefinition. Meaning and conventional function need not necessarily be linked. Buildings need to coax people back into working with them rather than against them ... they need a time dimension, a mental dimension ... or what we could call narrative.' This methodology can be seen to shift the emphasis of design away from being an internalised and essentially private language, allowing it to integrate into wider networks of cultural signification.

Fisher utilised this kind of approach when he was commissioned to design a new show for The Rolling Stones in 1989. At this time, the band had not played together live for seven years and wanted to create a performance environment that demonstrated their continuing relevance as they entered their third

decade together. During the 1960s, The Rolling Stones had occupied a central position in popular culture, and had played a significant role in defining contemporary style. This position was noted by cultural theorist Iain Chambers in his 1986 book *Popular Culture: The Metropolitan Experience*, in which an image of the cover of the Rolling Stones' second album for Decca appears as the frontispiece. The photograph itself, a moody black-and-white image of the band, was the work of David Bailey, a young photographer famous in his own right, who later provided the inspiration for Antonioni's cult film *Blow-up*. In Chambers' opinion, it was not the image itself that is important, but rather the fact that 'the group', their music, the album cover and the photographer stand together on the threshold of what *Time* magazine would later call 'swinging London'. Which is to say that together these elements represent a defining moment in an emerging cultural milieu.

THE 'EVENT AS CITY' USES URBAN FORMS AS NARRATIVE SIGNS

Event as city

In searching for an appropriate visual environment
for The Rolling Stones to serve as a reflection of both
their status and contemporary life in the late 1980s,
Fisher considered the transitional state that the western world had recently undergone, that has led to the
emergence of 'post-industrial' society. As a concept,
'post-industrial' can be characterised as a shift from
economies based on heavy industry and manufacturing, to those based on information and services. This
shift has precipitated a dramatic decline in the need
for manual labour, and an associated rise in employ-
ment connected to consumerism, leisure and entertainment, and with micro technologies.

The physical consequences of these changes had
already begun to affect film makers and writers, and
manifested themselves as apocalyptic visions concerned with urban decay and dystopian futures,
which captured the popular imagination, and formed
the cultural backdrop for Fisher's designs for what
became The Rolling Stones' 'Steel Wheels' tour.

Of particular interest to Fisher at this time were
the novels of William Gibson, including the *Sprawl
Trilogy* which launched a whole new subgenre of
science fiction known as cyberpunk. These writings
were generally concerned with the convergence of
technology and underground pop counter-culture,
set against a backdrop of social and urban decay. It is
interesting to note that cyberpunk itself was aligned
with rock music, a fact pointed out by Bruce Sterling
in his introduction to *Mirrorshades*, a collection of
cyberpunk stories in which he claims that 'the hacker
and the rocker are this decade's pop culture idols'.

The 'Steel Wheels' performance with downtown Los Angeles in the background. The show played across North America during 1989 and visited thirty-three cities over a fifteen-week period. The massive stage set was transported in 80 trucks and required a travelling crew of 200 people, with a further 150 hired locally for each performance.

To some extent this vision of the future was given visual form in film director Ridley Scott's *Bladerunner* which was released in 1982. In this film, the veteran product designer Syd Mead was given the role of 'visual futurist' and he began by envisaging a new cultural scenario based on specific social, economic and technological changes. The environments and products of the future were then designed in response to these shifts, which led to the idea of 'retro-fitting' in which old machinery and structures were not replaced, but simply upgraded using added-on elements. As a result, the environments of *Bladerunner* have a chaotic, multilayered and grimy look, which create the dark brooding atmospheres of *film noir*, and the alienated nocturnal urban interiors of Edward Hopper's paintings. This vision stood in stark contrast to the 1960s projections of the future which envisaged clean, bright and minimal utopian cities, and marks a clear shift from a modern to a post-modern aesthetic sensibility.

Working within this contemporary vision of the future, Fisher began the design process by showing The Rolling Stones a large image of the NASA launch platform with the shuttle removed, which he suggested belonged to a bygone age; representing the last vestiges of Victorian engineering. Such outdated or obsolete industrial forms litter the landscape of everyday life, and act as monuments to dead technologies. The gargantuan set (the largest touring stage ever built) which emerged from these early discussions drew upon the powerful forms of steel mills, refineries, oil rigs and power stations; the redundant technology of industries in decline, which were played back to the audience as a glamorised image. This huge structure invoked a sense of nostalgia for a bygone age which was particularly relevant to the baby-boomer generation who formed the original Rolling Stones fan base, and had witnessed this industrial decline at first hand.

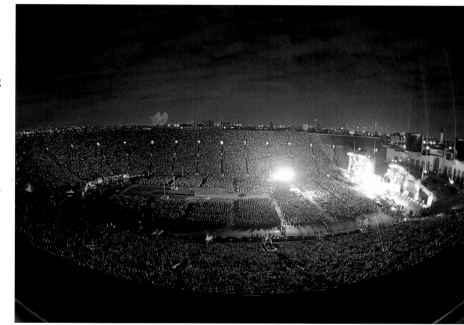

THE GARGANTUAN SET USED FOR 'STEEL WHEELS' WAS THE LARGEST TOURING STAGE EVER BUILT

Voodoo Lounge

By the time that The Rolling Stones began preparations for their next tour in 1994, many of the ideas and visual influences that had informed Fisher's designs for 'Steel Wheels' had been superseded by new cultural representations of the future. The cyberpunk genre of science-fiction writing had passed its peak, and the technologically dystopian visions of the future posited by films such as *Bladerunner* and *Brazil* were being replaced by more optimistic accounts of what commentators perceived as the emerging Information Age.

This transformation may be seen as a direct response to the actual technological advances that were taking place in the early 1990s. When the 'Steel Wheels' show was conceived in 1989, the Internet did not exist in any publicly recognisable form. By 1994, however, even though few people had direct access to these technologies, their existence and potential for instituting major shifts in the functioning of society were common knowledge. This realisation was essentially fuelled by the media, and in particular specialist magazines such as *Wired* which was launched in 1993 from the west coast of America, the location of 'Silicon Valley' and home to the majority of the world's leading software developers. Many of the articles in such publications evangelised the new technologies and the role they would play in transforming people's lives. This presented a compelling vision of the future questionable only by the fact that the major advertisers in these magazines tended to be those high-tech companies that sought to gain the most from its realisation.

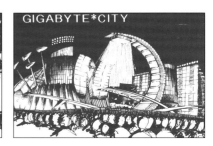

'Voodoo Lounge' took as its theme the information age, but had to rely on a historical 'Buck Rogers' vision of the future for its styling due to the lack of visual signifiers for what is essentially an invisible economy. The only exception to this is the @ symbol introduced by e-mail which has become a ubiquitous sign for anything remotely connected with the Internet or new media technologies.

Whatever the status of the impending Information Age – whether the logical next step for humankind, or cynical corporate hype – its cultural significance in 1994 meant that it provided an ideal basis for the new Rolling Stones' production. It also raised an interesting issue regarding the visual language of the stage environment. Whilst in the design of the 'Steel Wheels' set Fisher had been able to draw on the powerful industrial architectures of the nineteenth and twentieth centuries, this latest theme presented the impossibility of imaging a future in which the underlying economy is essentially invisible, and based on an ethereal flow of information rather than tangible manufactured products. Indeed, Fisher has observed that the only major visual manifestation of this new economy has been the @ symbol introduced by e-mail, which has become a ubiquitous graphic signifier for the Information Age. His response to this situation was to draw upon a 'historical' vision of the future as a basis for the design, creating a streamlined 'Buck Rogers-style' set which whilst today obviously representing a fantasy, still carries powerful connotations of a technologically mediated future for the audience.

Fisher gave the project the working title of Gigabyte City and the stage designs presented the audience with an alternative future, 'a place filled with computers in which people traffic in information'. The resulting stage design plays off harsh gridded metallic surfaces which resemble networks of electronic circuits, with flowing organic forms. A vast, apparently free-standing, facade wraps around the rear of the stage acting as a gleaming backdrop, and flanked by two 'technical silos' containing lighting rigs and the PA system. To the sides of the stage, gantries cantilever out above the audience and the whole ensemble is presided over by the menacing form of the 'Cobra', an expressionistic snake-like form clad in stainless steel providing further lighting positions and spectacular pyro-effects.

Whereas the 'Steel Wheels' set looked as if it had always existed, and that the band were performing in some previously abandoned industrial form, retro-fitted for the event, the 'Voodoo Lounge' resembled nothing on earth, an urban vision from a different age. Whilst these designs were being progressed, both Mick Jagger and the lighting designer Patrick Woodroffe suggested that the show needed a softer, more sensual mood for the middle section of the performance; an antidote to the clinical forms of the Gigabyte City-scape.

Working with a new title for the whole production, 'Voodoo Lounge', which had been suggested by band member Keith Richards, Fisher examined the social implications of technology, and in particular the deep-seated popular fear of the Information Age caused by an increasing abstraction and depersonalisation of the world. Of particular interest were the ways in which people attempt to overcome this 'techno-fear', often turning towards the mystical or

THE STAGE DESIGNS PLAYED OFF HARSH
GRIDDED METALLIC SURFACES WHICH
RESEMBLED ELECTRONIC CIRCUITRY
WITH FLOWING ORGANIC FORMS

The 'Voodoo Lounge' consisted of twelve inflatables that could be deployed in under thirty seconds. The bizarre cast included Durga, a Black Friar, Baron Samedi, a goat's head, an alarm clock, Elvis, a cobra, the Madonna, a one-armed baby and various assorted beads.

supernatural to defend themselves against an invisible technological force.

Amongst the many sources consulted, two in particular influenced subsequent design work. The first of these was a book entitled *Faces of God* which detailed through a series of essays and photographs the transfer of Voodoo practices from the Ivory Coast in Africa to the islands of the Caribbean. Amongst these were the creation of 'radio graves', in which 'wireless' technologies were incorporated into tombstones in the belief that they could open channels of communication with the dead. This remarkable socialisation of technology bore a strong relationship to an image Fisher had discovered in a book on catholic shrines found in dwellings in New Mexico. The image showed a broken TV set with the tube replaced by a group of plaster figurines, a religious scene elevated to the iconic status of the electronic image.

The designs that developed from this were illustrated in a series of collages, and became a disturbingly surreal inflatable tableau formed out of a series of incongruous icons: the 'Voodoo Lounge' of the show title, which including amongst other items a Hindu goddess, a Madonna, Elvis, a Black Friar, and an alarm clock. Fisher likens this symbolic environment to a suburban teenager's bedroom, which to the casual observer appears to have no overall coherence but actually represents an individual act of 'bricolage', a subjective system of selection which brings a highly personalised ordering to the world.

THE SURREAL TABLEAU OF 'VOODOO LOUNGE' WAS A SHRINE OF SENTIMENTAL ICONS

Bridges to Babylon

Having explored alternative visions of a technological future for the performance environments of 'Steel Wheels' and 'Voodoo Lounge', Fisher and The Rolling Stones turned their attention towards an altogether different yet extremely topical notion as the starting point for their next production: the impending *fin de siècle*. Historically, the end of a century in Western culture has often been associated with a period of decadence, an all-pervasive spirit of hedonism precipitated by a society acting in fear of the impending apocalypse.

Transforming this recurring *Zeitgeist* into a powerful visual form that could be communicated to an audience led Fisher towards ideas of opulence and flamboyance, and in particular to examples of excessive architectural ornamentation that often accompany displays of power and wealth. Religious buildings and artifacts provided an effective resource for

THE ICONOGRAPHY IN THE INITIAL DESIGNS WAS DRAWN FROM RELIGIOUS SOURCES

these visual signifiers and in particular the extraordinary decorative churches found in central South America, elements of the Vatican and examples of Bavarian Baroque architecture. In his early conceptual sketches, Fisher utilised aspects of these powerful cultural forms and combined them with other religious iconography such as crucifixes into extravagant performance environments. A second series of proposals retained some of these elements, but added forms drawn from other cultural sources including the elaborately carved stone temples of south-eastern India and the fantastic architectures produced through the obsessive desires of individuals, such as Ferdinand Cheval's 'Palais Idéal' (the so-called 'Postman's Palace' beloved by the Surrealists), and the exuberant forms of Watts Towers built between 1921 and 1954 by Simon Rodia in a suburb of Los Angeles.

The final designs for the tour shifted their frame of reference to more classical notions of opulence which were inspired by the name given to the album accompanying the Stones' tour: 'Bridges to Babylon'. This title suggested the transportation of the audience to a mythical place synonymous with both luxury and vice; the precise conditions that produce an atmosphere of decadence. As a consequence, the overtly religious motifs that dominated the earlier sketch proposals were replaced by more classical references including a massively overscaled Ionic

The approaching *fin de siècle* formed the starting point for the design of 'Bridges to Babylon', and the fact that the end of a century in Western culture has often been associated with a period of decadence, an all pervasive spirit of hedonism precipitated by a society acting in fear of impending apocalypse.

capital and giant Abyssinian columns which acted as supports for the huge female figures that reclined either side of the video screen. Flanking the stage, the symmetrical PA towers were modelled as gigantic golden torches swathed with rippling fabric, at the feet of which stood elaborate male and female figures, developed by Gerrard Howland of the San Francisco Opera and based on the dynamic sculptural forms of Umberto Boccioni.

The overscaled columns were introduced into the stage designs as the narrative shifted from overtly religious iconography towards more classical references. The complex papyrus bud capitals were based on actual designs used in Egyptian temples, and the truncated Ionic Column formed a plinth for the inflatable figure.

The columns were created out of standardised and custom-made components which were combined into severely distorted architectural forms. The papyrus bud capitals were manufactured out of GRP and the columns' shafts were made out of stretched fabric which could be quickly removed whilst the band were performing on the second stage in the middle of the audience.

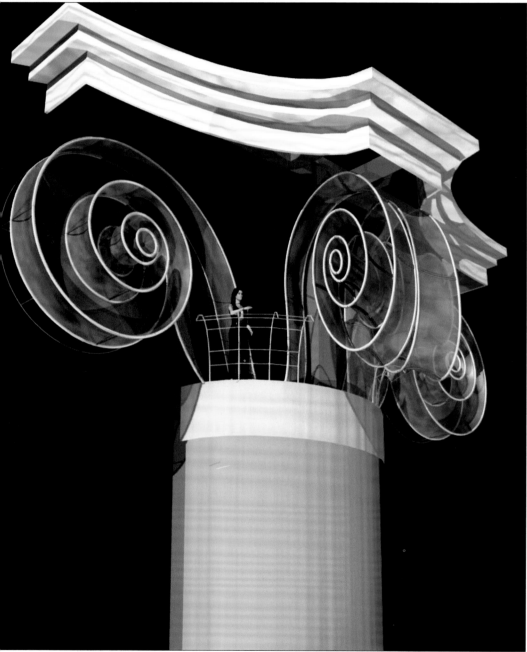 

Unlike previous shows designed by Fisher, the inflatable characters were not deployed in front of the audience but were already present on stage when the curtains fully opened, which gave them the appearance of being sculptures. These were removed while the band were off the main stage to give the set a stripped down appearance for the closing sequences of the show.

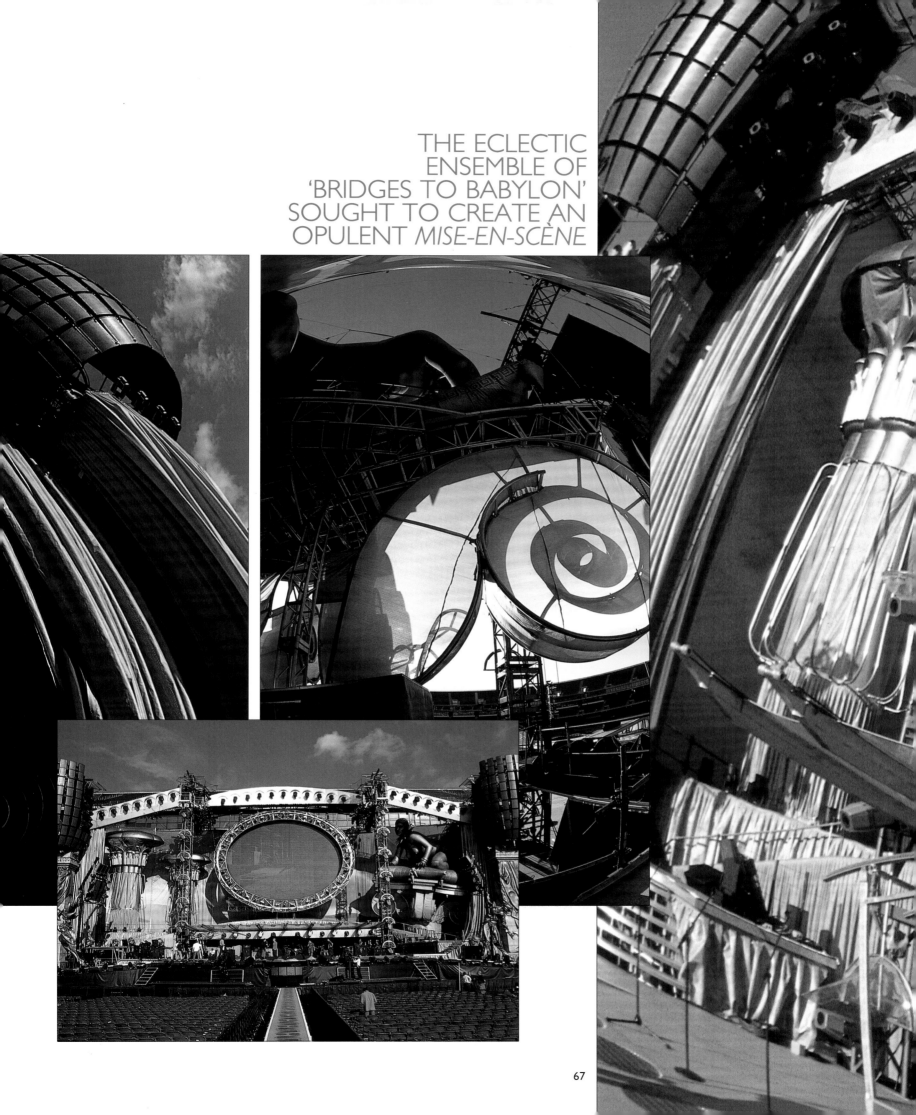

THE ECLECTIC
ENSEMBLE OF
'BRIDGES TO BABYLON'
SOUGHT TO CREATE AN
OPULENT *MISE-EN-SCÈNE*

IN HIS STAGE DESIGNS
FISHER INTEGRATES THE
LIGHTING FIXTURES INTO
THE ARCHITECTURAL FORM

70

Development of rock set lighting

The wildly eclectic ensemble of elements that made up the 'Bridges to Babylon' set did not seek to convey a specific story, but was more concerned with the creation of an opulent *mise-en-scène*, which was further enhanced by the sumptuous lighting effects of Patrick Woodroffe, with whom Fisher had previously collaborated on a number of shows, including 'Steel Wheels' and 'Voodoo Lounge'.

Woodroffe was introduced to the rock concert business during the 1970s by his brother Simon, who was at the time one of the few rock and roll stage designers in Britain. In these early days, fully fledged rock stage sets were virtually non-existent, and effects were generally produced by small unsophisticated lighting rigs which were operated by the companies who hired them out. During the 1970s, artists like David Bowie, Arthur Brown and Jimi Hendrix began to use more elaborate lighting effects for their performances, but it was not until the late 1970s that Heavy Metal bands began to utilise more extensive systems. By then, lighting designers had emerged as key to the whole production and effectively became, in the absence of any other elements on the stage, the designers of the show. Subsequent developments saw the introduction of scenic backdrops and drum-risers. As Bands became more willing to spend money on physical structures, the performance environment became more memorable.

Woodroffe cites Fisher's 'Steel Wheels' set of 1989 as marking a significant advance in the staging of rock concerts which had considerable implications for his own lighting designs. Previously, outdoor sets constructed in sports stadia had followed an extremely formulaic structure, consisting of a roof above the stage designed to provide shelter for lighting and performers flanked by PA towers. With The Rolling Stones show Fisher broke apart this relationship by dispensing with the roof altogether and creating for the first time a fully integrated design in which lighting fixtures became an important part of the structural and scenic elements of the rock set. The dramatic effect of this reconfiguration was to replace two-dimensional scenery with a three-dimensional object that created a more compelling context for the show.

This new concept of the 'stage as architecture' contained within it a paradox for lighting design, for whilst greater limitations were placed on the positioning of light fittings, this allowed the design itself to become more ambitious, hence presenting Woodroffe with a more extraordinary object to light. Such an approach demands a close working relationship between the two designers, and has led to a situation in which their individual roles during the development of a performance environment have become increasingly blurred.

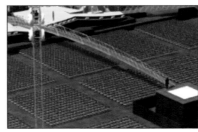

Show Dynamic

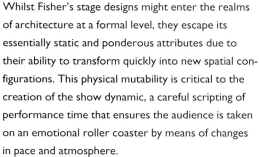

Whilst Fisher's stage designs might enter the realms of architecture at a formal level, they escape its essentially static and ponderous attributes due to their ability to transform quickly into new spatial configurations. This physical mutability is critical to the creation of the show dynamic, a careful scripting of performance time that ensures the audience is taken on an emotional roller coaster by means of changes in pace and atmosphere.

The structuring of a show has to take into account a myriad of variables including the pace and feel of any given song, the performers' movements, the stage setting and mood created by its lighting, and the use of any special effects such as video imagery or pyrotechnics. The show dynamic itself arises from the way in which all these elements interrelate at any given moment, and in particular how they develop over time and create an entire performance that is more than the sum of its parts.

During the ten years that Fisher and Woodroffe have collaborated on projects for The Rolling Stones, a very specific structure has emerged that provides the most comfortable format for the band to perform their material live in front of tens of thousands of people. This particular show dynamic follows the structure of a classical symphony in that the performance is generally divided into separate 'movements' which are clearly differentiated from one another but thematically linked. The stage sets play a major role in articulating this structure by being transformational, allowing the stage environment to be reconfigured for each section of the show. These metamorphoses, or 'reveals', are deployed at key moments in the performance adding a sense of drama to the occasion. Similarly, a series of spectacular one-off happenings (or 'gags' as they are known), which are related to specific songs, add individual high points within a given 'act'.

During the show's design development stage, the 'set' to be performed on tour will be relatively schematic, with just a few key songs at the start or

end of the show already fixed, leaving the majority of the performance to be sequenced later into a series of shifting musical tempos that provide the driving force behind the show dynamic. Once this outline structure of the performance has been completed and agreed with the band, the final designs are completed, and the physical elements of the set are assembled for rehearsals. When the set has been constructed, Woodroffe is able to experiment with the lighting effects on each of Fisher's environments, and creates a variety of moods and atmospheres which are then organised into a 'catalogue of potential looks', from which selections can subsequently be made. During this last stage of the design process the final set list is compiled by the band with input from both Woodroffe and Fisher, and an appropriate lighting atmosphere is assigned to each song which reinforces its mood, whether it be abrasive, melancholic, ecstatic, malevolent or any other emotion provoked in the listener as a result of the song's performance.

Since 1995, when digital video technology became affordable in a small studio, Fisher has been using 3D animation in the design process. This technique allows him to investigate the interaction between scenic elements in real-time, effectively modelling the show dynamic. Fisher observes that this approach shifts the attention of the designer away from static objects towards time-based activities, and as a role, closer to that of a director. Video animation is also a powerful means of communication for presentations to the band who are more familiar with TV as a medium than more traditional and static forms of architectural representation such as drawings and models.

THE USE OF 3D VIDEO ANIMATION
ALLOWS THE INTERACTION
BETWEEN SCENIC ELEMENTS
TO BE INVESTIGATED
IN REAL-TIME DURING
THE DESIGN PROCESS

A typical Rolling Stones show will commence with an extraordinary opening 'gag' that immediately grabs the attention of the audience and introduces the band, who will play five or six well-known, high-energy songs before slackening the pace. Lighting during this phase will generally start with brilliant white, revealing the stage architecture and band, before a limited palette of colour begins to be introduced. Then, just as the audience believe they have the measure of the setting, Fisher's stage environment will undergo its first big 'reveal' and transform into something more spectacular. This provides the theatrical help that the band require as they perform the first of their new songs, with which the crowd are less familiar.

About halfway through the show the set is subjected to its biggest metamorphosis, dramatically changing character, such as the moment in the 'Voodoo Lounge' when an inflatable shrine suddenly appeared in the midst of a hard crystalline cityscape. This section of the show often contains slower songs that lead up to the final section of the performance, referred to by Woodroffe as the 'home run'. During this phase the audience is treated to a series of the band's most famous songs, played at an ever increasing pace on a set stripped down to its most basic elements, but animated by frenzied lighting sequences, which culminate in a cataclysmic finale involving pyrotechnics: The Rolling Stones always go out with a bang.

This method of structuring the performance clearly informs the 'Bridges to Babylon' show, which begins with the building of a sense of anticipation from the moment the audience enter the stadium and are confronted with a set cloaked by curtains exuding a sense of mystery. The idea of shrouding the set was evident in Fisher's earliest proposals for the show, and although it changed in its physical articulation, remained as a key idea throughout the project development. During the opening sequence of the show, these curtains are partially drawn back to reveal only the elliptical video screen, whilst ominous pre-show music and lights played across the

heads of the audience enhance the general sense of anticipation. Finally, a small speck appears in the centre of the screen, the start of the opening 'gag', which turns out to be a flaming meteorite apparently hurtling towards the audience at an alarming rate. Just as this simulated televisual object appears to collide with the surface of the screen, special zero-residue 'laser rockets' mounted around the screen detonate and fire 30 metres into the air over the heads of the audience. The band, already on stage, strike up 'Satisfaction' and from this moment on the careful scripting of the show ensures that this will be guaranteed.

With masses of white light flooding the set and Mick Jagger's face dominating the stage on the overhead video screen, the band quickly establishes a rapport with their audience. Over the course of a few songs, the initial blistering pace of the show is slowed, before the first big transformation in the 'Bridges to Babylon' set, when the huge curtains are finally pulled back to reveal the full extent of the stage. The gigantic columns and draped PA towers turn the stage into a vast palace which responds to the scale of the stadium and is inhabited not only by the band but also the huge golden inflatable women and their front stage guardians, all sumptuously lit by Woodroffe in green and gold.

Halfway through the show, all the lights are extinguished and the eponymous 'Bridge' of the show title emerges from underneath the stage, cantilevering out over the audience some 40 metres to a second, smaller stage in the centre of the stadium. As the band traverse this heroic gesture, its metaphorical status also becomes apparent. The structure bridges the spectacular excesses afforded by their contemporary status in the rock world and

a representation of their more humble beginnings in the small clubs of London in the early 1960s. This modest platform, simply illuminated with white light, provides a setting for the band to recreate their early sound, a stripped down music with raw power, which is performed in a manner akin to the 'unplugged' sessions instigated by MTV in response to the criticism that too much contemporary music is overproduced and has lost touch with its basic origins.

This sudden display of intimacy in the midst of a vast spectacle produces a powerful sense of nostalgia for those who have literally grown up with the band, a reaffirmation of their original identification with its values, as well as affording an unexpected insight into a previous incarnation of the group for those too young to have witnessed it for themselves. The simplicity of this interlude in a simulated past also serves to heighten the drama of the final 'home run' sequence of show. The band returns to the main stage which has been stripped down to its basic elements. The inflatables and rear wall have been removed, allowing the last phase of the performance to be illuminated from behind. The closing numbers, 'Honky Tonk Woman', 'Start Me Up', 'Jumping Jack Flash' and 'Brown Sugar' are accompanied by an ever increasing spectacle of lighting and special effects. This includes the blowing of vast quantities of tickertape into the audience which produces a sense of carnival, a riotous celebratory atmosphere that culminates in a cataclysmic display of fireworks as the band leave the stage and the stadium is plunged into darkness.

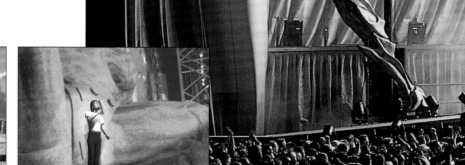

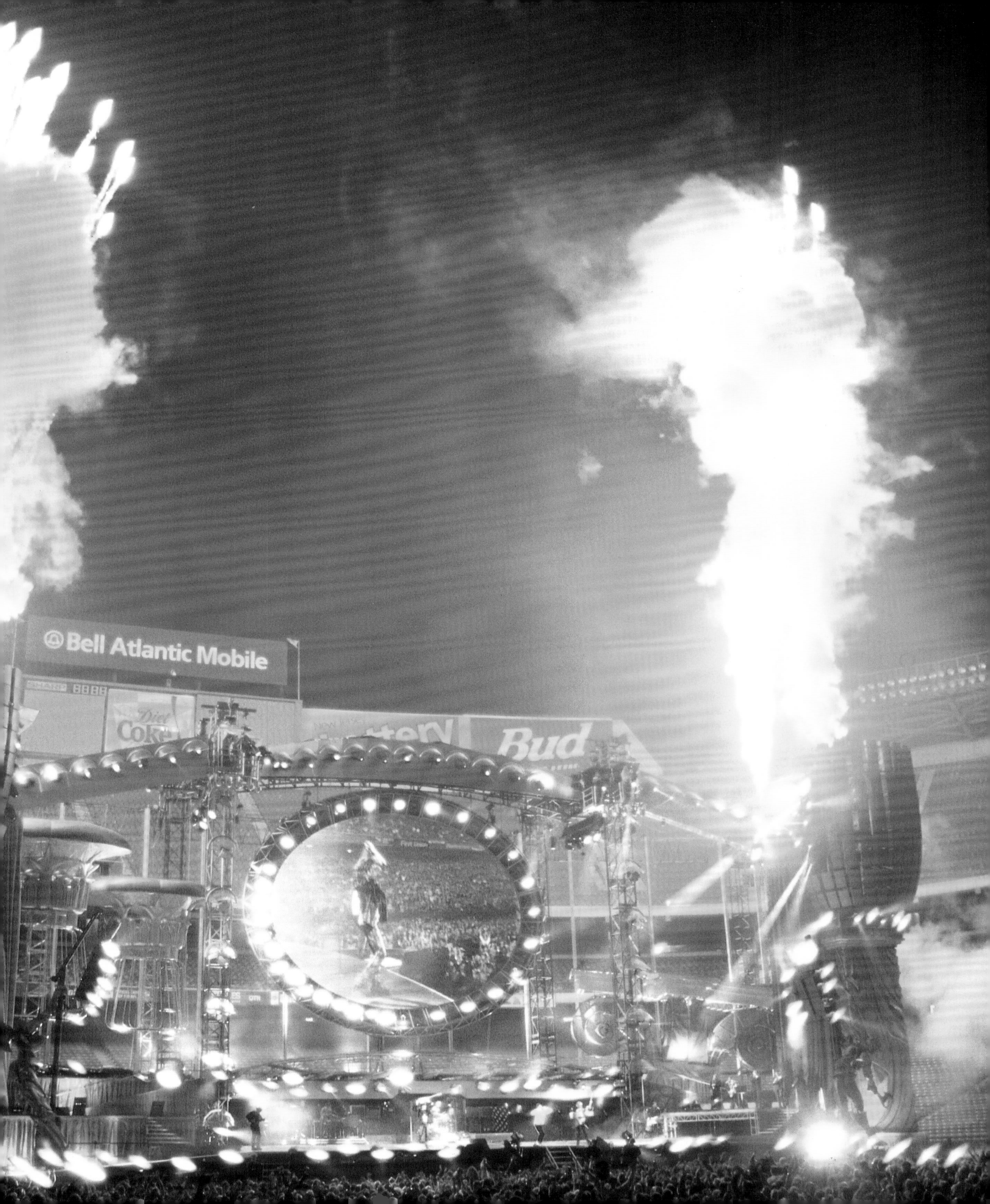
Bell Atlantic Mobile
Bud

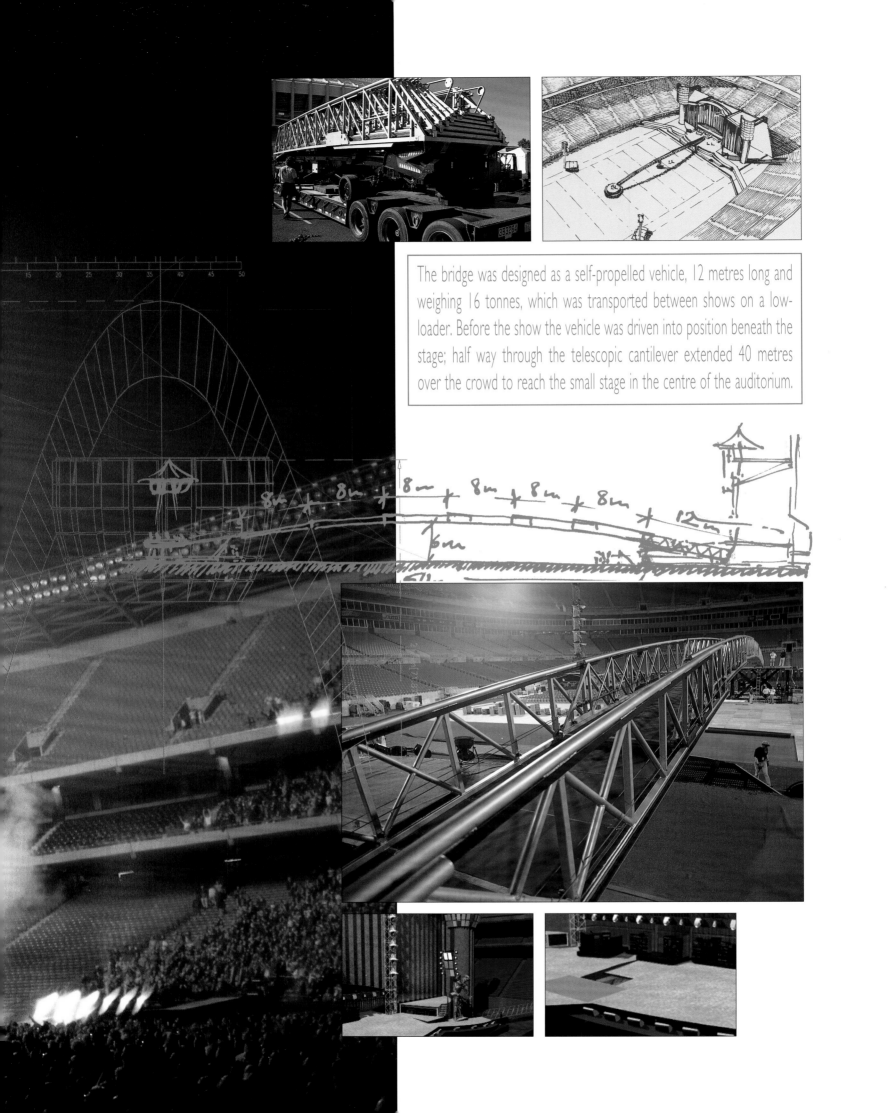

The bridge was designed as a self-propelled vehicle, 12 metres long and weighing 16 tonnes, which was transported between shows on a low-loader. Before the show the vehicle was driven into position beneath the stage; half way through the telescopic cantilever extended 40 metres over the crowd to reach the small stage in the centre of the auditorium.

THE STRUCTURE SERVED A
METAPHORICAL PURPOSE BRIDGING
BETWEEN THE SPECTACLE AFFORDED BY
THE BAND'S CURRENT STATUS AND A
REPRESENTATION OF THEIR HUMBLE
BEGINNINGS IN SMALL CLUBS

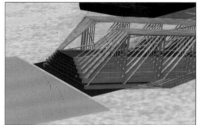

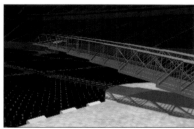

Spontaneity vs the script

Predetermining the exact format of a show dynamic would appear to be at odds with the immediacy and spontaneity that characterise live performance as opposed to recorded music. Woodroffe argues that, paradoxically, the more spontaneous the performance, the less spectacular a show can be. This is due to the fact that in order to be used spontaneously, the stage set, lighting and special effects would have to be more generic because they cannot be programmed to heighten the experience of specific songs.

However, repeating the same show, no matter how spectacular, for the duration of an entire tour, runs the risk of both the band and production team becoming bored, with the inevitable consequence of less stimulating performances. For this reason, a number of techniques are utilised to help mitigate against these circumstances. The first of these concerns the individual songs that are played in the show. Whilst some of these are fixed and constitute important 'production numbers' or pieces that allow the performance to shift tempo, others are chosen for their particular mood, and can be substituted with others of a similar nature without disturbing the overall show dynamic, thus keeping the set list in flux and ensuring that every night is a special occasion. This strategy of allowing for a degree of spontaneity in the show is also carried over into the technical side of the production. Since the advent of sophisticated computer technologies, entire sequences of lights that accompany songs can be blocked out and triggered by a single cue. This makes for a prosaic experience for those operating the lighting rig, so Woodroffe tries to strike a balance between pre-programming complex lighting sequences and some live operation of lights, which leaves the technical staff with a sense of direct involvement.

Both Fisher and Woodroffe are aware that whatever their individual and collective contributions are to a show, the most important element of all is the performance of the band itself, and that even the most spectacular staging cannot act as a substitute for the emotional charge generated by the charisma of individual performers. Unlike Pink Floyd, where the focus of the band's performance is primarily concerned with a display of cerebral atmospheric music, The Rolling Stones focus on attitude. This is more in keeping with Jagger's status as an archetypal 'rock-god' whose mere presence on stage is enough to incite the crowd into a paroxysm of excitement. Jagger uses his cultural standing as leverage in live performance, 'working' the audience through a series of gestures, vocal inflections ('Wow!'), direct conversation ('Hey ... <insert appropriate city> ... are you feelin' alright?'), costume changes and energetic movements around the stage. In this way, according to Woodroffe, Fisher's sets function as a 'kinetic playground' for Jagger with extended side areas and galleries placed at higher levels to allow the performer to interact with different sections of the crowd.

This psychological bonding has the knock-on effect of producing what Fisher describes as a 'tribal identity'; the shared experience of a vast crowd all focused on the activity of a single shaman-like individual. This is witnessed in the many ways in which the crowd respond, with communal singing, screams and shouts, which lie outside normal emotional behaviour and are found elsewhere only at large sporting events and religious meetings. The show structure itself takes account of this gradual establishment of a relationship between the band and audience by the way in which the theatrical sets which are present at the start of the performance are gradually stripped away to leave just the band as the focus of attention.

Video as a magnifying technique

One increasingly significant factor in maintaining this performer/audience relationship during a rock show has been the introduction of the video screen. The utilisation of this technology is in part a direct response to the shift in the locations used for rock concerts, from the intimate yet inappropriately genteel ballrooms and dancehalls of the 1960s to the monstrous impersonal spaces of sports stadia. In this transition, a fundamental dimension of performance was lost from the rock concert: namely the ability of the audience to see the facial expressions of those on stage, making an intimate atmosphere practically impossible. Video technology attempts to restore this relationship and functions as a scaling device that mediates between the insignificant physical presence of the performer on stage and the vast expanses of the venue. The band are no longer tiny specks on a vast stage, but appear quite literally 'larger than life'. They are given physical proportions commensurate with their celebrity status; intimacy becomes part of the spectacle. Video technology augments the visual experience and magnifies key features of the performers, such as the unflinching stare of Watts, the craggy smile of Richards, and Jagger's trademark pouting lips, thereby extending the physical attributes of performance into the realms of the televisual.

With video cameras on stage constantly moving around and a live editing process taking place, the images on the screen above the stage do not actually represent what is happening below. Rather, they are intensified media constructions, which use technological effects to heighten the experience of the audience. This makes watching the show a more complex exercise involving a constant switching between the physicality of the 'live' performance and the mediated or 'relayed' images on the screen. This blurring of reality and representation serves ultimately as a useful reminder of the nature of stardom or celebrity itself, as the archetypal 'rock-god' is, after all, part physical presence and part media construction.

VIDEO CAN BE USED TO RESTORE THE INTIMACY OF FACIAL GESTURES THAT HAVE BEEN LOST IN STADIUM SHOWS

Logistics

Although an audience may leave a concert exhilarated by the performance of the band and the spectacular accompanying visual effects, other logistical factors play an important role in determining the overall success of a rock show. The majority of outdoor concerts are held in sports stadia which can accommodate large audiences but which have no technical facilities for staging concerts. The presentation of a touring show therefore requires the construction of a temporary building which provides weather protection for the band and supporting structures for sound, lights and scenery. A large stage structure such as that used in 'Bridges to Babylon' can take up to five days to construct and dismantle. With the financial investment in large scale stadium rock concerts running at up to $1 million per show, three or four performances are required each week in order to make a tour economically viable. These will often take place in different cities up to 400 miles apart, which creates a demanding timetable that cannot be achieved by simply moving the entire show from stadium to stadium in a linear sequence.

This logistical problem is usually overcome by dividing the components of the show into two parts: a high-tech assemblage which includes all the custom-built decorative elements, video, sound and lighting; and a low-tech portion comprising the supporting structure. The short life of even the largest rock tour means that capital costs must be amortised over a few months. To keep the capital costs down, only the decorative elements and essential connecting structures are custom-built, whilst all the other high-tech components and the low-tech steelwork systems are rented.

Outdoor sports stadia can accommodate large audiences but have no technical facilities for staging concerts. The presentation of a touring show therefore requires the construction of a temporary building to provide weather protection for the band and supporting structures for scenery and technical equipment such as the sound and lighting.

Two or three sets of the steelwork structure are taken on tour at the same time, and leap-frog between cities. During the three days preceding each concert, these are erected by small travelling crews assisted by local labour. This strategy minimises the transport and construction costs, which together account for a large proportion of the total production budget.

In the early days of stadium concerts, the stage structures were often assembled from conventional construction industry scaffolding. However, as the touring rock show business has grown, specialised international staging companies such as the Belgium based StageCo and London based ESS have developed proprietary steelwork systems which are faster to erect. The components are specifically manufactured for portability and ease of handling, and typically consist of modular trusses which are designed to fit inside one another and pack efficiently on trucks. They also employ water-ballasted bases and self-erecting tower systems. All the proprietary staging systems available for hire are designed to form simple box-like buildings with flat roofs supported by flanking towers for PA and video. Much of Fisher's work has involved finding ways of reconfiguring these basic systems into supporting frameworks for more complex structures.

The custom-built scenery and high-tech components are transported to the stadium directly from the previous show, often arriving on the morning of the performance. In a few hours they are rigged to the pre-built structural framework by a specialist team who tour with the show. Besides functioning as a symbolic visual environment, the scenery is designed in the knowledge that its rapid deployment and disassembly is one of the most critical operations in the programming of the tour. Just as the band rehearse material for the live shows in the weeks leading up to the start of a tour, so the production crew will practise the critical 'loading in' and 'loading out' of the set. In this way they perfect the 'choreography of construction' that is required to

THE CHOREOGRAPHY OF CONSTRUCTION ENSURES THE DELIVERY OF 3 OR 4 SHOWS PER WEEK

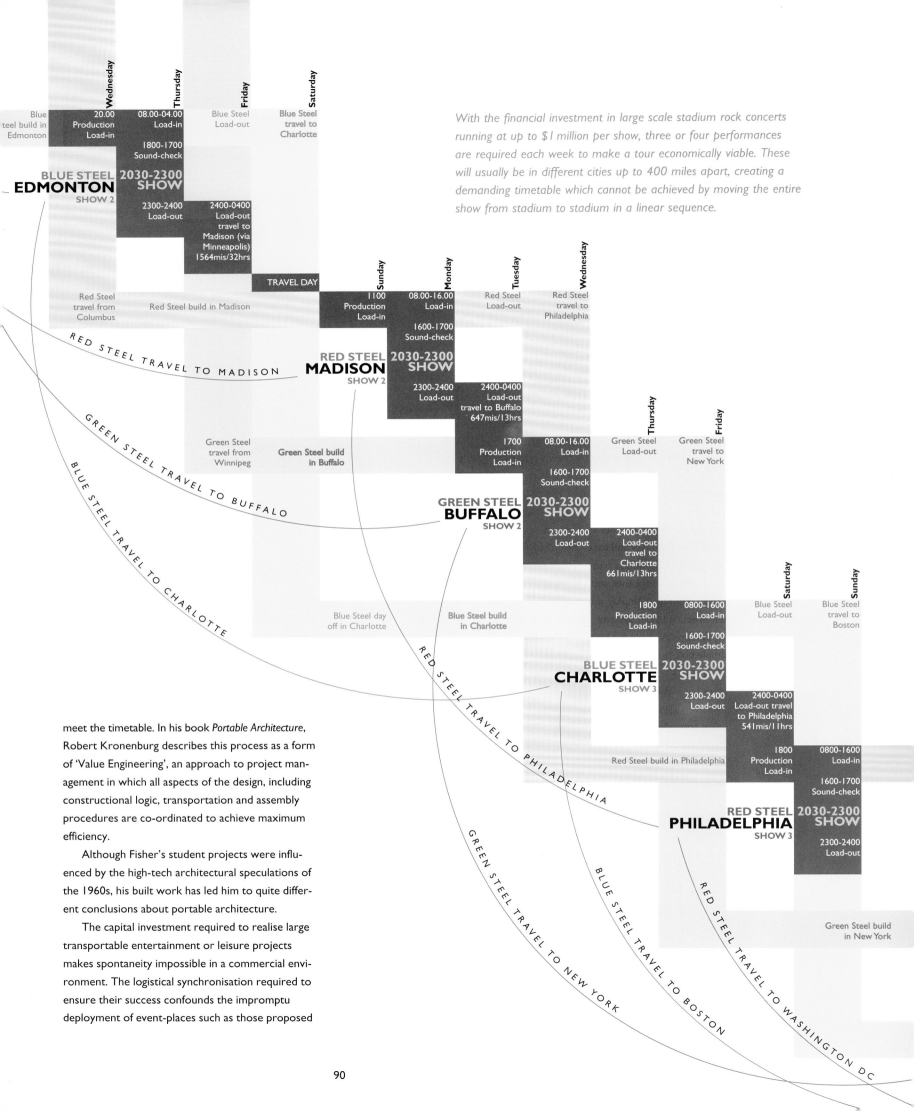

With the financial investment in large scale stadium rock concerts running at up to $1 million per show, three or four performances are required each week to make a tour economically viable. These will usually be in different cities up to 400 miles apart, creating a demanding timetable which cannot be achieved by moving the entire show from stadium to stadium in a linear sequence.

meet the timetable. In his book *Portable Architecture*, Robert Kronenburg describes this process as a form of 'Value Engineering', an approach to project management in which all aspects of the design, including constructional logic, transportation and assembly procedures are co-ordinated to achieve maximum efficiency.

Although Fisher's student projects were influenced by the high-tech architectural speculations of the 1960s, his built work has led him to quite different conclusions about portable architecture.

The capital investment required to realise large transportable entertainment or leisure projects makes spontaneity impossible in a commercial environment. The logistical synchronisation required to ensure their success confounds the impromptu deployment of event-places such as those proposed

BLUE STEEL EDMONTON — SHOW 2

- Wednesday / Thursday / Friday / Saturday
- Blue steel build in Edmonton
- 20.00 Production Load-in
- 08.00-04.00 Load-in
- 1800-1700 Sound-check
- 2030-2300 SHOW
- Blue Steel Load-out
- Blue Steel travel to Charlotte
- 2300-2400 Load-out
- 2400-0400 Load-out travel to Madison (via Minneapolis) 1564mis/32hrs
- TRAVEL DAY

RED STEEL MADISON — SHOW 2

- Red Steel travel from Columbus
- Red Steel build in Madison
- Sunday / Monday / Tuesday / Wednesday
- 1100 Production Load-in
- 08.00-16.00 Load-in
- 1600-1700 Sound-check
- 2030-2300 SHOW
- Red Steel Load-out
- Red Steel travel to Philadelphia
- 2300-2400 Load-out
- 2400-0400 Load-out travel to Buffalo 647mis/13hrs

GREEN STEEL BUFFALO — SHOW 2

- Green Steel travel from Winnipeg
- Green Steel build in Buffalo
- 1700 Production Load-in
- 08.00-16.00 Load-in
- Thursday / Friday
- 1600-1700 Sound-check
- 2030-2300 SHOW
- Green Steel Load-out
- Green Steel travel to New York
- 2300-2400 Load-out
- 2400-0400 Load-out travel to Charlotte 661mis/13hrs

BLUE STEEL CHARLOTTE — SHOW 3

- Blue Steel day off in Charlotte
- Blue Steel build in Charlotte
- 1800 Production Load-in
- 0800-1600 Load-in
- Saturday / Sunday
- 1600-1700 Sound-check
- 2030-2300 SHOW
- Blue Steel Load-out
- Blue Steel travel to Boston
- 2300-2400 Load-out
- 2400-0400 Load-out travel to Philadelphia 541mis/11hrs

RED STEEL PHILADELPHIA — SHOW 3

- Red Steel build in Philadelphia
- 1800 Production Load-in
- 0800-1600 Load-in
- 1600-1700 Sound-check
- 2030-2300 SHOW
- 2300-2400 Load-out
- Green Steel build in New York

RED STEEL TRAVEL TO MADISON
GREEN STEEL TRAVEL TO BUFFALO
BLUE STEEL TRAVEL TO CHARLOTTE
RED STEEL TRAVEL TO PHILADELPHIA
GREEN STEEL TRAVEL TO NEW YORK
BLUE STEEL TRAVEL TO BOSTON
RED STEEL TRAVEL TO WASHINGTON DC

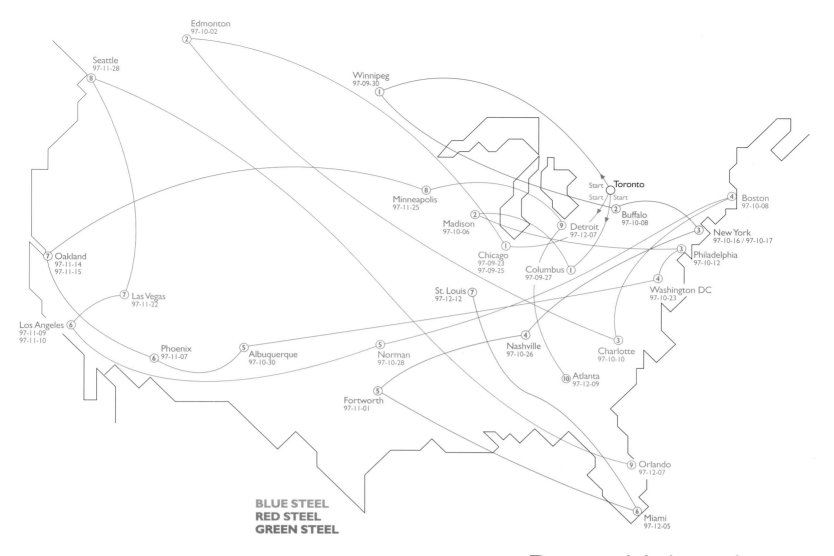

Edmonton
97-10-02
②

Seattle
97-11-28
⑧

Winnipeg
97-09-30
①

Start Toronto Start
Start   Start

⑧ Minneapolis
97-11-25

Boston
97-10-08
④

Madison
97-10-06
②

⑨ Detroit
97-12-07

Buffalo
97-10-08
②

New York
97-10-16 / 97-10-17
③

⑦ Oakland
97-11-14
97-11-15

Chicago
97-09-23
97-09-25
①

Columbus
97-09-27
①

③
Philadelphia
97-10-12

⑦ Las Vegas
97-11-22

St. Louis
97-12-12
⑦

Washington DC
97-10-23
④

Los Angeles
97-11-09
97-11-10
⑥

Phoenix
97-11-07
⑥

⑤ Albuquerque
97-10-30

Norman
97-10-28
⑤

Nashville
97-10-26
④

Charlotte
97-10-10
③

⑩ Atlanta
97-12-09

Fortworth
97-11-01
⑤

⑨ Orlando
97-12-07

BLUE STEEL
RED STEEL
GREEN STEEL

⑥ Miami
97-12-05

Monday

Red Steel
Load-out

Tuesday

Red Steel
Travel to
Washington DC

2400-0400
Load-out travel
to New York
538mis/10.5hrs

DAY OFF

Wednesday

Thursday

1800
Production
Load-in

0800-1600
Load-in

1600-1700
Sound-check

GREEN STEEL   2030-2300
NEW YORK   SHOW
SHOW 3

Blue Steel
3 days off in Boston

Blue Steel build in Boston

Brand Identity

by Archigram in projects like 'Instant City'.

A further difference between the idea and the reality of portable architecture can be observed in the aesthetics of the high-tech architectural 'style' when applied to movable buildings. The speculations of architects such as Richard Horden and Jan Kaplicky frequently annexe design elements from high-performance aerospace and marine vehicles. The elements are recycled as stylistic devices which carry connotations of portability to more mundane applications. Fisher notes that truly nomadic architectures such as circuses and rock shows deal with the technical issues of portability without celebrating them as an aesthetic. Indeed, in his stage designs for The Rolling Stones, the use of urban forms engenders an atmosphere of permanence that plays with the audience's subconscious understanding of the rock show as a temporary environment. It is an approach that disregards the functionalist approach to form making, freeing the rock set to become a symbolic environment for communication with the audience.

This self-conscious 'styling' of a performance environment is important not only because it connects into wider networks of cultural signification, but also because the functional differences between individual designs are essentially small. With only a stage, a lighting system and a decorative set as design elements, superficial but deliberately exaggerated stylistic differences become critical in differentiating one rock show from another. Fisher likens this approach to product branding, which has influenced the management of large rock bands since the mid-1980s, as the entertainment industry has become a part of the global economy. In this system of entertainment commodities, the rock concert becomes the 'live product' of the band, and its 'style' contributes significantly to their 'brand identity'.

The management of a 'brand' in rock music, like that of other commercial activity, is concerned with the projection of a unique and consistent identity to the consumer. This emanates from the ethos of the producer (the band) and defines the characteristic 'feel' of their products, including their recorded music, live performance, packaging and merchandising. Occasionally, however, groups institute wholesale changes to their identity as they explore new

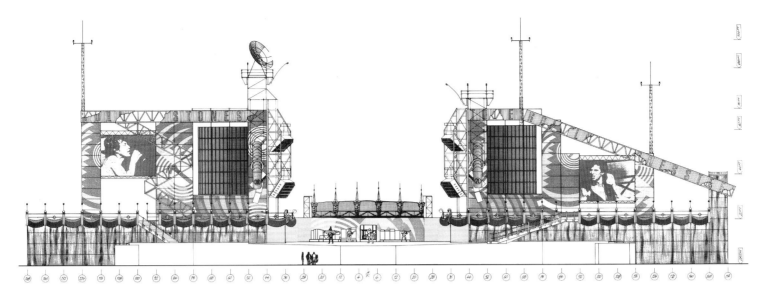

Rolling Stones *Steel Wheels* 1989

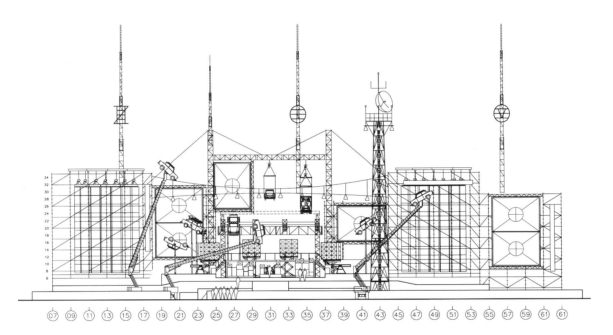

U2 *ZOOTV* 1992

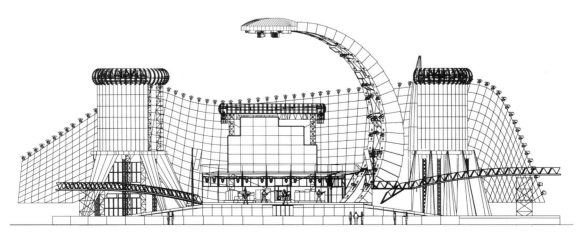

Rolling Stones *Voodoo Lounge* 1994

50m

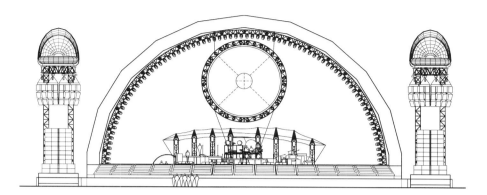

Pink Floyd *Division Bell* 1994

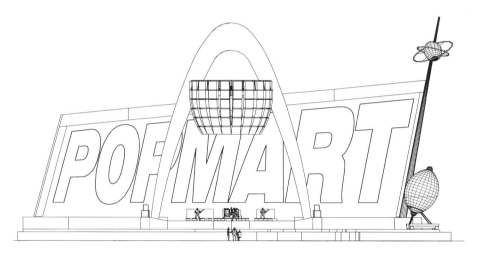

U2 *POPMART* 1997

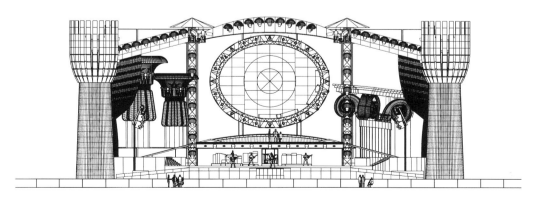

Rolling Stones *Bridges to Babylon* 1997

50m

creative avenues. The work carried out for U2 by Fisher in collaboration with the show designer Willie Williams since the early 1990s illustrates this process. The band have used their live performances as a way of underlining the change in direction that was taking place within their music.

During the 1980s, U2 brought out a series of increasingly successful and critically acclaimed albums which combined classic rock with punk and Gaelic influences. The lyrics that accompanied their brooding and insistent music often expressed social and political concerns which added gravity to the individual songs and gave the band a sense of authenticity that appeared to transcend their status as a market commodity.

This creative approach reached its apotheosis with 'The Joshua Tree' album of 1987, and was accompanied by a performance that reflected the 'no nonsense' philosophy of the band at the time. Willie Williams, the designer of the show, described his approach as 'an exercise in minimalism', in which he reacted against the extravagant technology that had begun to dominate lighting design. In contrast to the excessive spectacles of bands like Genesis and Pink Floyd, Williams' approach was simple and direct. He used man-operated follow spots to focus the crowd's attention on the performers themselves, creating an understated mood that resonated with the band's social and political consciousness.

The success of 'The Joshua Tree' and its associated tour led U2 to be acclaimed both 'Band of the Eighties' by *Rolling Stone* and 'Rock's Hottest Ticket' by *Time* magazine. At the moment they reached this pinnacle of achievement, however, the band decided that they needed a new creative direction that was radically different from the sobriety and earnestness of their early work. This shift in attitude was reflected in their subsequent studio recordings, including 'Achtung, Baby' which was released in 1991 and the 'Zooropa' album of 1993, both of which featured a more complex sound and a less politicised lyrical content. Whilst these releases represented a significant departure for the band, it was in the live performances that accompanied them that the full extent of their reinvention became most apparent, and in particular the 'ZooTV' extravaganza.

93

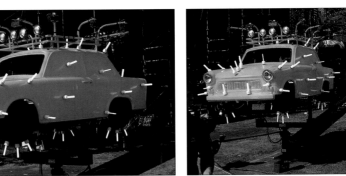

THE SHOW WAS DESIGNED TO GIVE AN
EXPERIENCE SIMILAR TO SURFING
CABLE TV CHANNELS

ZooTV

The 'ZooTV' project appeared radically different from earlier live performances by U2 due to its reliance on video for visual effects. The decision to use this medium was partly due to Williams' concurrent work with REM, who had pioneered the use of video in live performance, but also to recent technological advances which were making it possible to project bigger and brighter images.

In his designs for the show, Williams was keen to exploit the full potential the medium offered and to extend it well beyond the simple close-up images of the band members. This approach typified the contemporary use of video in rock shows, and Williams felt it was too limited. He was highly critical of the fact that this new technology had been added to traditional set and lighting design without much consideration of how it affected the dynamics of the performance space. Williams was also aware that even the most rudimentary use of video required a full studio to be taken on tour, and believed that this facility could be exploited to achieve something far more ambitious.

During Williams' early conversations with the band, Bono, the lead vocalist, suggested that they should effectively take a TV station out on tour, and deliver an experience similar to flicking through the multiple channels of cable TV. Williams responded to this idea by creating a performance in which the audience were bombarded by 'sustained video chaos'. This visual imagery slipped in and out of synch with the subject matter of individual songs, creating sudden moments of lucidity counterposed with contradictory statements or random streams of consciousness.

Williams' show for 'ZooTV' began as a tour of indoor venues, but as the performances moved into larger outdoor sports stadia, Fisher Park were invited to collaborate due to their experience of staging larger rock events. This change of scale brought with it an entirely new series of discussions regarding the nature of the performance environment, which ended with the band expressing a preference for an 'undesigned' set that should either look unfinished, or as though it had been left behind from another event and reused by U2.

Fisher responded to this difficult proposition of creating a self-conscious 'non-design' by using scaffolding to screen the vast PA system, and designing a series of telescopic lighting pylons which resembled radio antennae or floodlighting structures, complete with built-in aircraft warning lights. These structures gave the stage a sense of impermanence that was reinforced by exposed lighting gantries and industrial luminaires located above the stage. Around the stage, banks of TV monitors and different sized projection screens were 'arranged' in a haphazard manner in order to disassociate the audience's perception of the video imagery from the passive experience of watching television.

Williams' lighting designs for 'ZooTV' continued his previous *ad hoc* use of found objects and modified domestic appliances as light fittings, but raised it to a new level by employing twelve customised Trabant cars that had been acquired in East Germany following the fall of the Berlin Wall. These were transformed into lighting instruments by Light & Sound Design of Birmingham, England, and the resulting contraptions were slung from gantries located above the band and mounted on grove lifts at the side of the stage from where they could be swung out above the crowd. The Trabant lights contributed a dynamic physical element that reinforced the driving music of the band and the frenetic video imagery, which when seen together resembled a delirious outside broadcast unit, or in Williams' own words 'a TV station in a blender'.

Although the 'ZooTV' show was extremely successful and critically well received, the band's change of direction gave some cause for consternation amongst their die-hard fans, who saw the show as evidence that the band had sold out their original values and had become another commodified product in 'mainstream' popular culture. In reality, this apparent loss of authenticity could not have been further from the truth, as the 'ZooTV' project can actually be seen as an attempt to circumvent this situation and address what might be a more authentic approach to rock performance in the media-saturated cultural landscape of the 1990s. Indeed, given the commercial success of the band by the end of the 1980s, it was already questionable whether the fans' perception of U2 as 'the voice of social and political consciousness' carried more weight as an authentic value system or as a powerful identity that was capable of being used for the marketing of the band's products.

It is important to note that this tension between creative integrity and commercial exploitation is not peculiar to the work of U2, but has always existed at the heart of rock music, which emerged in direct response to the market demand for 'youth culture'. In recent times, this tension has been intensified by the increasing role given to the visual image in the promotion of rock music, and in particular the explosive growth in the use of video.

Television has always played an important part in the dissemination of rock music, and its emergence as a ubiquitous consumer technology in the early 1960s has been deemed a significant factor in the rapid early growth of its market. Until the start of the 1980s, rock music tended to be presented to the TV viewer in the form of studio performances, which were recorded in front of audiences of young people and attempted to recreate the atmosphere of live concerts. The introduction of video radically altered this situation by co-opting techniques from film or television itself, adding stylised settings, visual effects and scripted narratives to the 'performance' of the music by the band.

The use of this medium for promoting rock music increased dramatically during the 1980s following the launch of MTV, a channel dedicated to popular music. MTV relied upon music videos almost exclusively for its programming, repeating newly released or successful material on a regular basis in the same manner as a radiostation playlist. The success of this channel has led to many imitations of its format, and to a situation in which the visual image now plays a fundamental role in consumers' perception of rock music, previously a primarily aural experience. Indeed, today it is practically unknown for material to be released without an accompanying promotional video, and the success of individual songs often appears to be as dependent on stimulating visual material as it is to the distinctive quality of the music itself.

Although the 'image' of individual rock bands has been carefully controlled throughout the short history of this cultural phenomenon, the use of video has not only increased the frequency with which bands are encountered visually, but also provides a powerful means through which their image can be controlled or constructed. This intensified mediation of a band's identity for commercial purposes raises the problem of authenticity and has led cultural theorist Lawrence Grossberg to suggest that within this new visually biased economy '... the only possible claim to authenticity is derived from the knowledge and admission of your own inauthenticity'. As a result, he observes that to operate with any degree of integrity, it has become 'increasingly important for performers and directors to incorporate signs of their ironic cynicism' within their creative activities.

This type of self-reflection was exercised at its most blatant level in U2's 'ZooTV' show in the way that Bono assumed an alter-ego, the gold-suited MacPhisto. During the band's performance in Sydney, this absurd character, a remix of the Devil and Elvis Presley, is heard to address the crowd and tell them in a bored tone, 'Look what you've done to me ... you've made me very famous and I thank you'. Whilst this added a touch of wry humour to the proceedings, it also allowed the singer to break a taboo, and express the unspoken truth behind the audience/performer relationship.

Actions such as this destabilise the 'real' identities of individual band members and raise questions as to whether 'Bono' (real name Paul Hewson) and 'The Edge' (David Evans) might also be assumed personalities, whose attitudes and concerns are purely 'staged' for the duration of the performance, and differ greatly from their 'real' personae.

This critical strategy was also applied in Williams' 'video chaos', which bombarded the audience with overwhelming amounts of visual imagery, and a series of provocative and often contradictory statements which flashed across the screens: 'YOU ARE A VICTIM OF YOUR TV'; 'DO NOT ACCEPT WHAT YOU CANNOT CHANGE'; 'EVERYTHING YOU KNOW IS WRONG'; 'WATCH MORE TV'; 'IGNORANCE IS BLISS'; 'BELIEVE EVERYTHING'. Williams' approach represented an intensification of the assault on people's senses performed by mass media in the course of everyday life, and its apparent refusal to yield any overriding message. This was in effect a 'wake-up call', designed to stir the audience out of passive consumption and force them into thinking for themselves. In this respect, 'ZooTV' can be read as a critique of mass media, and in particular the way in which television, newspapers and advertising condition thought and make people conform to the rules of the political establishment, whilst simultaneously creating a desire for the consumer products that fuel its economy.

Fisher's stage designs reinforced this message by resembling a mobile TV outside broadcast unit, leaving the audience unsure as to whether they were the recipients of a live performance, or were in fact a studio audience providing the atmosphere for an event being transmitted elsewhere. The success of Fisher's performance environment in achieving this ambiguous state is perhaps best judged by the way in which it appears to integrate with the landscape of the sport stadia itself, with existing advertising hoardings and floodlighting appearing to form a part of the overall schema.

This blurring of the distinction between what constitutes 'reality' and what is 'media construction' that occurred throughout the 'ZooTV' project ultimately related to wider debates taking place at the time concerning postmodern culture, and in particular the theory of 'hyperreality' put forward by the French sociologist Jean Baudrillard. Hyperreality, which Baudrillard perceives as representative of our current state of 'being in the world', is seen as

inextricably linked to the increasing influence of advertising, media and communication networks, which have become the essential sphere for human understanding and dialogue. Within a postmodern world, the image of an object or event assumes a greater importance than knowledge of the thing or occurrence itself, and is consumed as a 'simulacra', or simulated experience of reality. In Baudrillard's view, no external reality now exists outside this system and everyday life is defined only by varying levels of simulation. This condition is reflected upon in U2's ironic paean to hyperreality, 'Even Better than the Real Thing', which made its appearance on the 'Achtung, Baby' album and concerns itself with the tendency within consumer culture for the reality of a thing to be inflated by cynical image marketing.

It is interesting to compare the approach of U2 in 'ZooTV' with that of Pink Floyd in the 'Division Bell', as both attempt in extremely different ways to extend consciousness and heighten the audience's experience of live performance. In the case of the latter, this is achieved by the utilisation of surreal and psychedelic imagery which are combined to invoke a dream-like state, whereas for U2, the torrent of information that constantly bombards the observer creates a sense of over-stimulation which is further enhanced by the dizzying mental effect of constantly blurring image and reality.

FOR STABILITY - 6 OR 10 LINES OF LED'S
@ 10mm C/C APPROX 1400 LEDS

BLADES DEPLOYED & STIFFENED BY
CENTRIFUGAL FORCE AS HUBS ROTATE
CARBON FIBRE BLADES AEROFOIL SECTION

6m

12m

REV APPROX
200 RPM

LED'S
ACTIVATED
BY
RADIAL
SECTOR

The Virtual
Ferris Wheel

The Virtual
Metronome

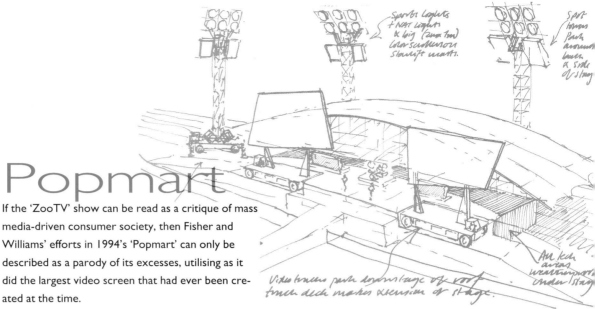

Video towers park downstage of roof truss deck makes extension of stage.

Popmart

If the 'ZooTV' show can be read as a critique of mass media-driven consumer society, then Fisher and Williams' efforts in 1994's 'Popmart' can only be described as a parody of its excesses, utilising as it did the largest video screen that had ever been created at the time.

Even while 'ZooTV' was still on tour, the band had already decided that they didn't want the show to be seen as a one-off event. Yet the sheer spectacle of the performance raised the difficult question of how this might be followed by something even more remarkable. As a consequence, when the band announced that they were to record a new album, Fisher was invited by Williams to collaborate with him on the design of the accompanying show. Initially their work focused on a range of possibilities which was created independently before being combined for discussions with the band.

Amongst Williams' suggestions for the show was 'The Bunker', a brutal monolithic structure resembling a military installation which was to have opened during the performance to reveal a contrasting interior that used video or soft visual elements and stood in stark contrast to its coarse exterior. A second idea featured a gigantic wave poised above the band that looked as though it was about to crash down and consume the stage, pierced by a series of enormous microphones positioned at curious angles.

What is interesting about these early proposals is their wide ranging and seemingly arbitrary nature, as the designers explore different possibilities before a clear sense of direction is established. This can also be observed in Fisher's initial sketches for the show which included a response to Williams' idea for a mobile discotheque, and consisted of a traditional stage inhabited by eight vehicles, four of which supported video screens and the rest lighting towers. It

FISHER PUT FORWARD A PROPOSAL TO TOUR WITH THE LARGEST TV EVER SEEN

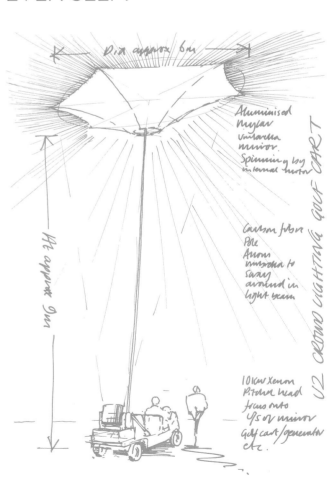

The final scheme began to emerge after Willie Williams coined the phrase **'POPMART'**. Fisher responded by sketching a supermarket-like building with the word written above its entrance. This image triggered the conceptual framework for the show which became a satire on *fin-de-siècle* consumer decadence.

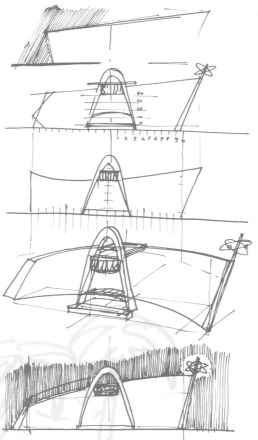

was proposed that during the show the band would move to a second position in the centre of the arena, and that these trucks would leave the main stage and take up positions within the audience, creating a performance in the round. Fisher went on to produce further designs for other vehicles that utilised LED, Light Emitting Diode 'signalman' technology which allows messages to appear as though they are written in the air. These devices were scaled up by Fisher and christened The Virtual Ferris Wheel and The Virtual Metronome.

Eventually one of Fisher's schemes called The Big Picture provided the basic form for the show and featured a vast LED screen assembled as video pixels, which were to be attached to a flexible mesh and draped over the seats at one end of the stadium. Creating a video screen on this scale only became possible during the conceptual stages of the project in early 1996, when a Taiwanese company overcame the limitations of LED technology by manufacturing an affordable blue video pixel to complement the red and green versions already commercially available. Fisher recognised the potential of this development and put forward an audacious proposal for the band to tour with the largest TV screen ever seen.

Further elements of the final design emerged after the band revealed that the title of their new album was to be 'Pop'. In response, Williams coined the word 'Popmart' and Fisher drew a sketch of a supermarket with the word written above its entrance. This simple image provided the show with

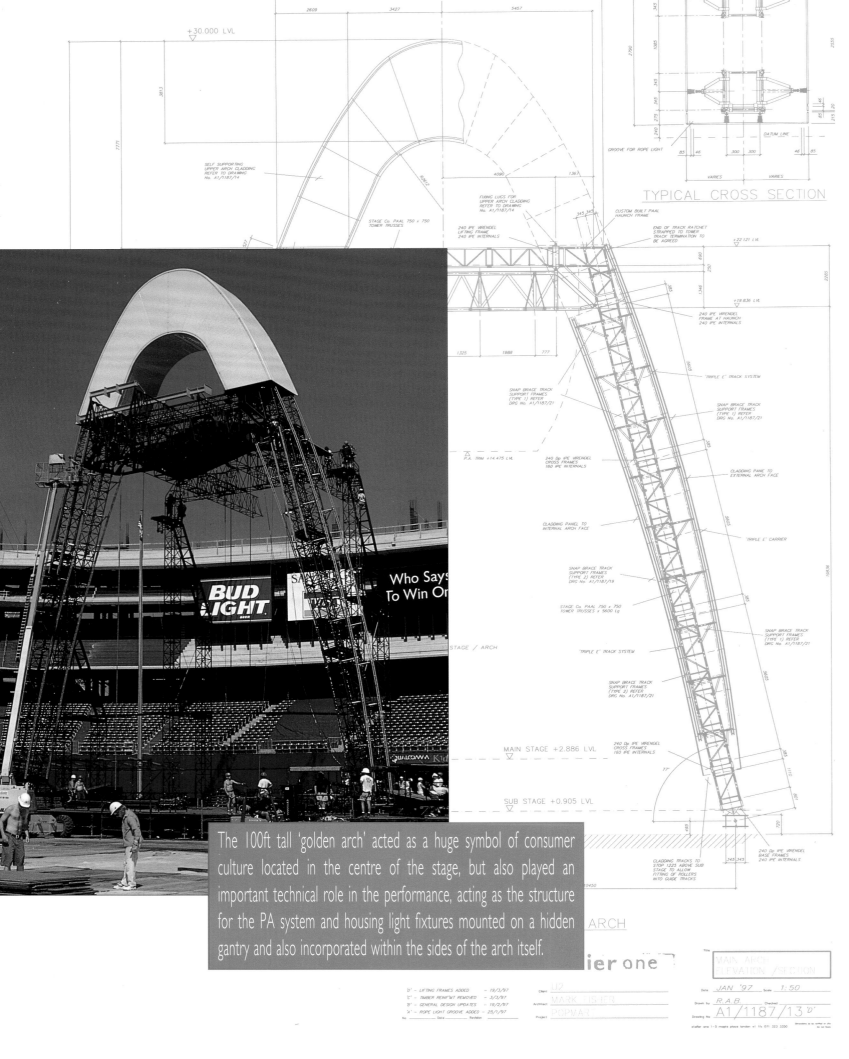

+30.000 LVL

SELF SUPPORTING
UPPER ARCH CLADDING
REFER TO DRAWING
No. A1/1187/14

STAGE Co. PAAL 750 x 750
TOWER TRUSSES

FIXING LUGS FOR
UPPER ARCH CLADDING
REFER TO DRAWING
No. A1/1187/14

240 IPE WRENDEL
LIFTING FRAME
240 IPE INTERNALS

CUSTOM BUILT PAAL
HAUNCH FRAME

END OF TRACK RATCHET
STRAPPED TO TOWER
TRACK TERMINATION TO
BE AGREED

+ 22 121 LVL

TYPICAL CROSS SECTION

GROOVE FOR ROPE LIGHT

DATUM LINE

VARIES   VARIES

+19.836 LVL

240 Dp IPE WRENDEL
FRAME AT HAUNCH
240 IPE INTERNALS

'TRIPLE E' TRACK SYSTEM

SNAP BRACE TRACK
SUPPORT FRAMES
(TYPE 1) REFER
DRG No. A1/1187/21

SNAP BRACE TRACK
SUPPORT FRAMES
(TYPE 1) REFER
DRG No. A1/1187/21

P.A. TRIM +14.475 LVL

240 Dp IPE WRENDEL
CROSS FRAMES
180 IPE INTERNALS

CLADDING PANE TO
EXTERNAL ARCH FACE

CLADDING PANEL TO
INTERNAL ARCH FACE

'TRIPLE E' CARRIER

SNAP BRACE TRACK
SUPPORT FRAMES
(TYPE 2) REFER
DRG No. A1/1187/19

STAGE Co. PAAL 750 x 750
TOWER TRUSSES x 5600 Lg

SNAP BRACE TRACK
SUPPORT FRAMES
(TYPE 1) REFER
DRG No. A1/1187/21

STAGE / ARCH

'TRIPLE E' TRACK SYSTEM

SNAP BRACE TRACK
SUPPORT FRAMES
(TYPE 2) REFER
DRG No. A1/1187/21

MAIN STAGE +2.886 LVL

240 Dp IPE WRENDEL
CROSS FRAMES
180 IPE INTERNALS

SUB STAGE +0.905 LVL

CLADDING TRACKS TO
STOP 1225 ABOVE SUB
STAGE TO ALLOW
FITTING OF ROLLERS
INTO GUIDE TRACKS

240 Dp IPE WRENDEL
BASE FRAMES
240 IPE INTERNALS

ARCH

ier one

The 100ft tall 'golden arch' acted as a huge symbol of consumer culture located in the centre of the stage, but also played an important technical role in the performance, acting as the structure for the PA system and housing light fixtures mounted on a hidden gantry and also incorporated within the sides of the arch itself.

'D' – LIFTING FRAMES ADDED – 19/3/97
'C' – TIMBER REINF'M'T REMOVED – 3/3/97
'B' – GENERAL DESIGN UPDATES – 19/2/97
'A' – ROPE LIGHT GROOVE ADDED – 25/1/97
No.   Date   Revision

Client
U2
Architect
MARK FISHER
Project
POPMART

Title
MAIN ARCH
ELEVATION /SECTION

Date   JAN '97   Scale   1:50
Drawn by   R.A.B.   Checked
Drawing No
A1/1187/13 'D'

THE BOLD FORMS
AND EXUBERANT
COLOURS MADE
REFERENCE TO
THE CONSUMER
ARCHITECTURE OF
MORRIS LAPIDUS

its conceptual framework: a satirical view of *fin-de-siècle* consumer decadence, in which 'Popmart' functioned as an 'entertainment outlet'. In his development of this theme, Fisher consciously referred to the work of Morris Lapidus and Raymond Loewy, two designers who rose to fame in the United States during the 1950s with design work directly related to the emerging culture of consumerism.

Lapidus was an aspiring actor before training as an architect at Columbia University, and went on to develop his reputation in the 1930s and 1940s, designing a series of innovative shop interiors in New York. These exploited his extensive knowledge of stage set design, and used bold forms, strong colours and atmospheric lighting to create highly stylised 'theatres of consumption'.

From the early 1950s Lapidus worked on a series of hotels in and around Miami including Eden Roc and most famously The Fontainebleau, whose sweeping streamlined curves and exotic interiors have featured as a setting for many films. This is not surprising since Lapidus' approach to the design of hotels was to conceptualise them as a series of spaces to be experienced as a cinematographic location, thereby responding to ordinary people's desire for the luxury and glamour associated with the cinema, rather than with the dour European modernity that was influencing architectural design in the United States at this time. Inevitably, this led to Lapidus' work being universally condemned by critics as vulgar, despite its overwhelming popularity with hotel customers. Fisher himself is no stranger to this particular form of criticism, in which high cultural values are used to judge designs created for a mass market, an approach which trivialises the important role such designs play in peoples' everyday

lives, and which reduces the debate to questions of taste.

Similarly, despite his huge success in the United States, the product designer Raymond Loewy is also reported to have received a negative response to his work from European critics, especially in Germany where the morality of his highly stylised designs was seen as problematic. Loewy's phenomenal success in the United States has been attributed in part to his understanding and exploitation of the 'replacement market' for goods which developed in the early 1950s. The consumer boom that followed the Second World War, as young couples set up homes and began to have children, stimulated the economy of the United States until the late 1940s, after which point an artificial demand had to be created for

consumer products. This 'replacement market' saw
the introduction of product design strategies such as
built-in obsolescence, the addition of 'new features',
and the use of styling as a method of product differentiation, which created further demand due to
changes in fashion.

Loewy's contribution to product design itself
was founded on his belief that user satisfaction was
derived more from the seductive power of the arti-
fact than from its pure utilitarian efficiency. His signature style of 'streamlining' originated in his designs
for vehicles, in particular cars and trains, which were
shaped to create lower wind resistance. This 'style'
was subsequently applied to a much wider range of
objects which had no functional need for streamlining, such as radios and other domestic appliances,
and this 'look' quickly established itself as a visual signifier of the future. Indeed, the ubiquity of the
streamline aesthetic in the 1950s has led François
Burkhardt to suggest that it functioned as a cultural
leitmotif which 'expressed the public's desire to
overcome the economic and social frictions of the
depression, (and) to flow through time with as little
resistance as a teardrop auto through air'.

Like Loewy's work, Fisher's final proposals for
the 'Popmart' show appeared deceptively simple, and
turned technical necessities such as the PA system
and video screen into bold visual forms. Likewise,
the product designer's characteristic 'streamline'
styling is deliberately employed by Fisher in the
design of the main elements of the stage, whose
sleek forms were further emphasised during the performance by having their edges outlined with neon
striplights. This was most apparent in the vast
50-metre x 16-metre LED video screen used to

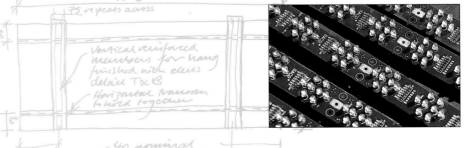

simple forms of both the 30-metre high golden arch that dominated the centre of the stage, and the PA system mounted upon it. The arch itself alluded to the corporate logo of a well-known fast food chain, and began life as a doodle drawn by Williams. As the theme of the show shifted towards being a satire on consumption, Fisher returned to this highly charged cultural motif and integrated it into the stage environment where it resonated with the audience at a subliminal level.

The overall simplicity of Fisher's final designs fulfilled Williams' desire for 'Popmart' to be perceived as the antithesis of 'ZooTV', both in terms of implied meaning and visual complexity. The positioning of the PA system above the centre of the stage, rather than to its sides, played an important role in creating a general sense of openness. This was further enhanced by the decision to use the video wall for illuminating the performance space and integrating more traditional lighting gantries and secondary light sources almost imperceptibly into the arch and screen structures.

The visual dominance of the screen in 'Popmart' meant Williams' use of video as a means of mediating between the band's music and the physical environment of the show assumed a much greater importance than had been the case with 'ZooTV'. His approach to video in both shows had its roots in Performance Art and Conceptual Installation, and was primarily influenced by the work of Laurie Anderson and Bill Viola, who combine arresting imagery with intellectual rigour whilst keeping their pieces accessible to their audience. For Williams, the work of these artists stood out from the majority of gallery-based video installations which he perceived as lacking in technical and conceptual quality, being either too esoteric or too banal.

DURING THE DAYTIME THE VIDEO WALL ALSO PARODIED ADVERTISING BILLBOARDS

create the rear wall of the stage, which was given a dynamic tilted shape by Fisher. This strategy not only differentiated it from more traditional rectangular formats of TV and cinema, but also meant that 'Popmart' achieved the first seamless integration of video technology into the physical architecture of a performance environment.

Along one of its sides, the massive video wall appeared to be held in position by a ludicrous 30-metre high cocktail stick spearing an olive. This visual element recalled Morris Lapidus' penchant for using thin decorative columns or 'beanpoles' as dramatic accents, and also served as a reference to the cocktail lounges of his Miami Beach hotels. Elsewhere, the design language of Lapidus, which has become synonymous with consumer environments, is reflected in Fisher's exuberant use of colour and the bold

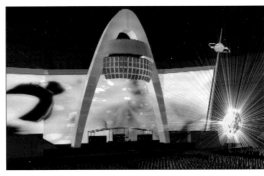

THE CAMERAS ON
STAGE PICKED UP
THE IMAGE ON THE
SCREEN BEHIND
THE BAND AND
SET UP A VISUAL
FEEDBACK LOOP

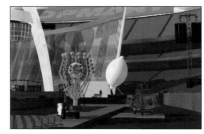

This general lack of innovation in the field of video art – with the exception of Anderson and Viola – could also be seen to characterise the use of video in rock performance, where it generally featured simply as a magnifying technology for delivering 'close-ups' of the band on stage. Although Williams acknowledges that the audience has literally paid to 'see' the band in these vast stadiums and that the video director is therefore almost duty-bound to relay these images, he also points out that these become dull when they are not integrated with other material. The insertion of video art into a live rock scenario is not without its own dangers, however, as the audience only sees this imagery once, and if it is not immediately comprehensible the video director risks losing their attention or making them feel intellectually inadequate. This possibility has to be measured against the use of clichéd or over-familiar imagery which can also annoy the crowd and leave them yearning for more close-up shots of the band.

Whilst these issues demand shrewd judgements to be made by the artist, by far the most difficult problem to be overcome in performance video is the fact that if an audience is presented with conventional imagery the show can rapidly become a passive experience like watching TV or going to the cinema. This is not only an inappropriate response to elicit in the consumption of 'live' entertainment, but also engenders the 'greatly reduced sense of wonder' that Williams maintains exists today. He believes this to be a result of the excessive use of computer effects in film and television, which have left the viewer blasé about what is seen on the screen no matter how spectacular it is. Williams argues that,

IN WILLIAMS' UNIQUE APPROACH TO VIDEO, HE SPATIALISES THE EXPERIENCE AND BRINGS VIEWERS INTO A PHYSICAL RELATIONSHIP WITH WHAT THEY ARE WATCHING

conversely, three-dimensional objects such as Fisher's 'Popmart' arch can have a far greater impact on the viewer's experience due to the fact that it is a 'real' experience rather than an illusory or virtual one. This theory underpins Williams' approach to performance video in which he spatialises the experience and brings viewers into a physical relationship with what they are watching. This is achieved by creating arrangements of screens that destroy their naturalised status as 'windows into another world', causing them to be perceived as multi-faceted and reprogrammable 'image objects' which have an ambiguous status that shifts between being a surface and being a space. These elements put pressure on the traditional notion of the 'lightshow', and could be used to add colour or texture to the performance environment, convey messages or images of the band members, or other imagery associated with the songs. This approach can be observed in both 'ZooTV' and 'Popmart', but whereas the former used multiple screens for video projection and banks of TV monitors, the latter employed one vast wall.

A further point of difference between the two shows was the resolution of the images themselves, which in 'Popmart' was considerably lower due to the decision to 'explode' the screen and move the video pixels a long way apart. A virtue was made of this by using bold simple images which drew on Pop Art. This visual reference reinforced the theme of the show, as its aesthetic was derived from the commercial art of product packaging and other forms of consumer culture during the late 1950s and early

The video screen was constructed out of more than 1 000 000 separate LEDs which are coloured by using exotic metals. During the design stage Fisher and Williams decided to 'explode' the screen by spacing apart the individual video pixels. This technique gave the show its particular aesthetic which was derived from the use of low resolution imagery

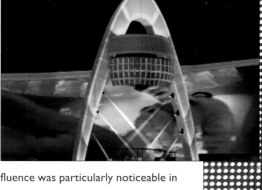

1960s. This influence was particularly noticeable in the treatment of the live material shot from the front of the stage, which was made more interesting for the audience by being highly stylised, using bold primary colours and multiple copies of the same shot in homage to Andy Warhol's artistic treatment of film and pop stars in the 1960s. The massive scale of the video wall meant that this documentary material picked up the image displayed behind the band members and set up a visual feedback loop. Although Williams was aware that this was likely to happen, it was impossible to know how this might look until the screen was built. As it turned out, the magnified LED pixels were largely responsible for the characteristic look of the show, and a deliberate colour cast was constantly used to heighten this effect. In addition to live feeds from roving cameras on stage, other material was inserted into the show. This was created by a number of artists whose innovative work was uncovered during a six-month period of research by Catherine Owens, who collaborated on 'Popmart' as curator of video material.

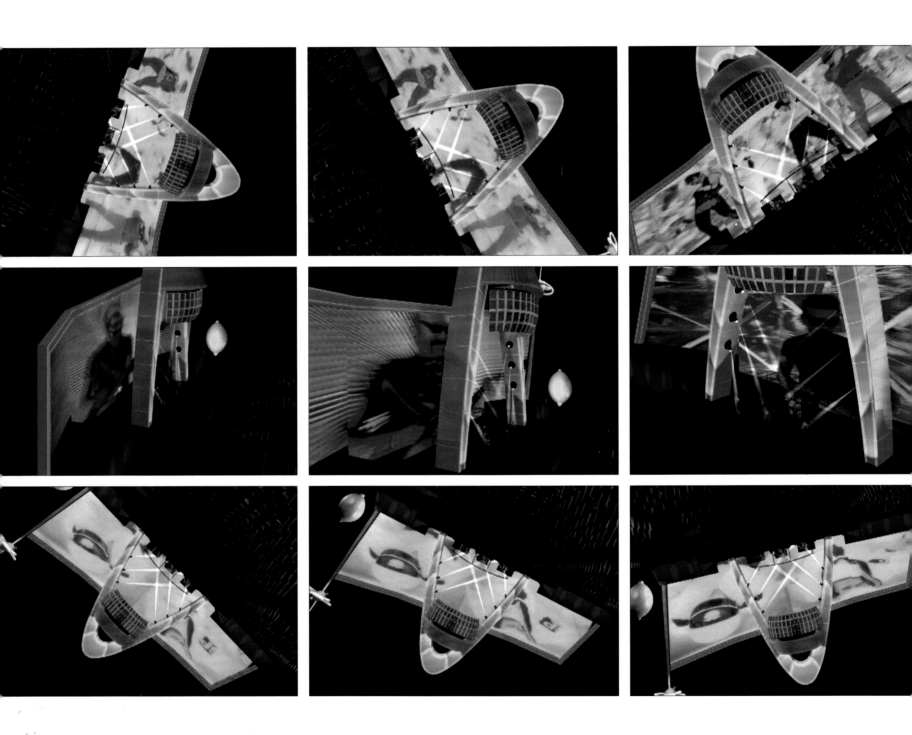

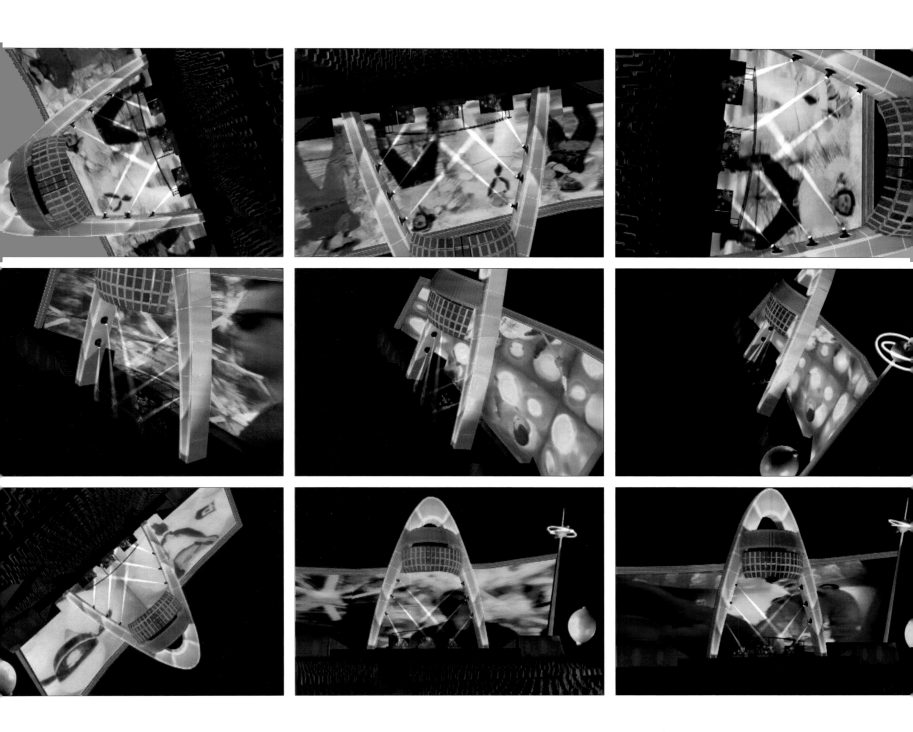

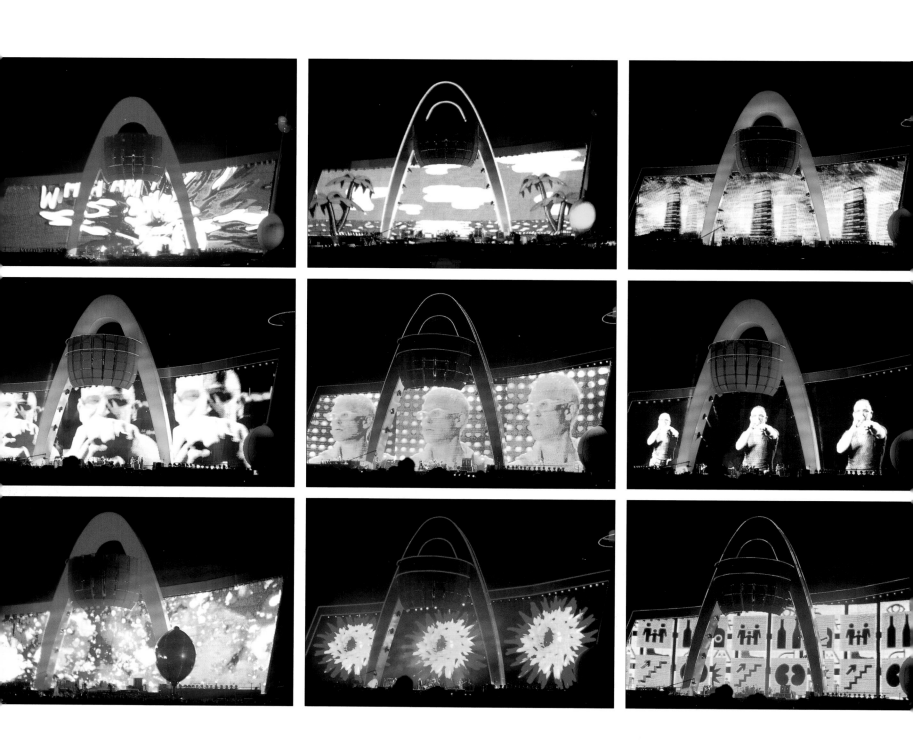

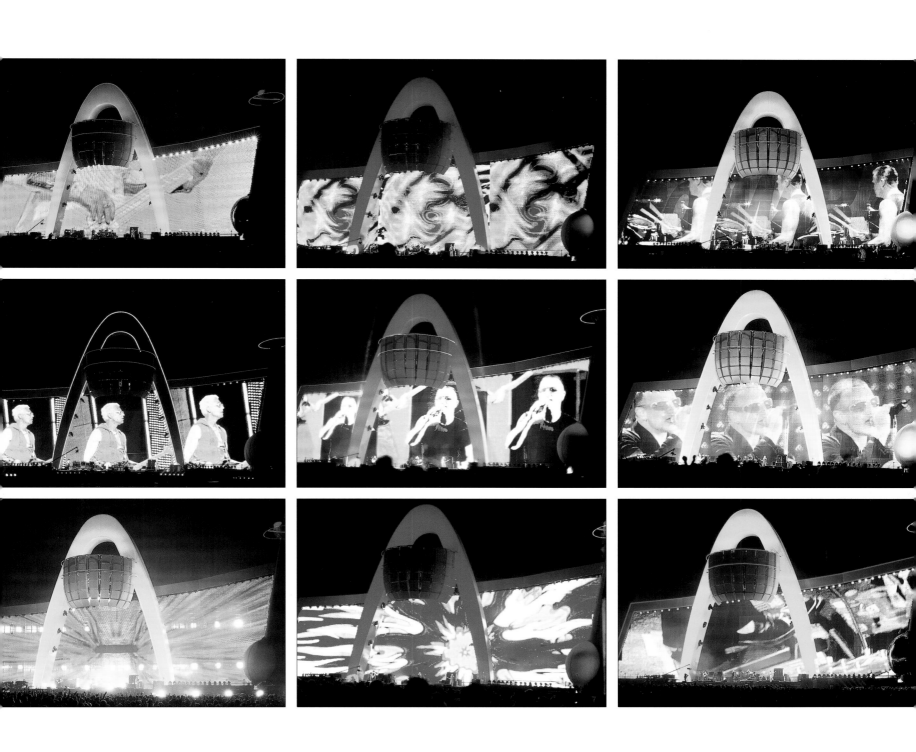

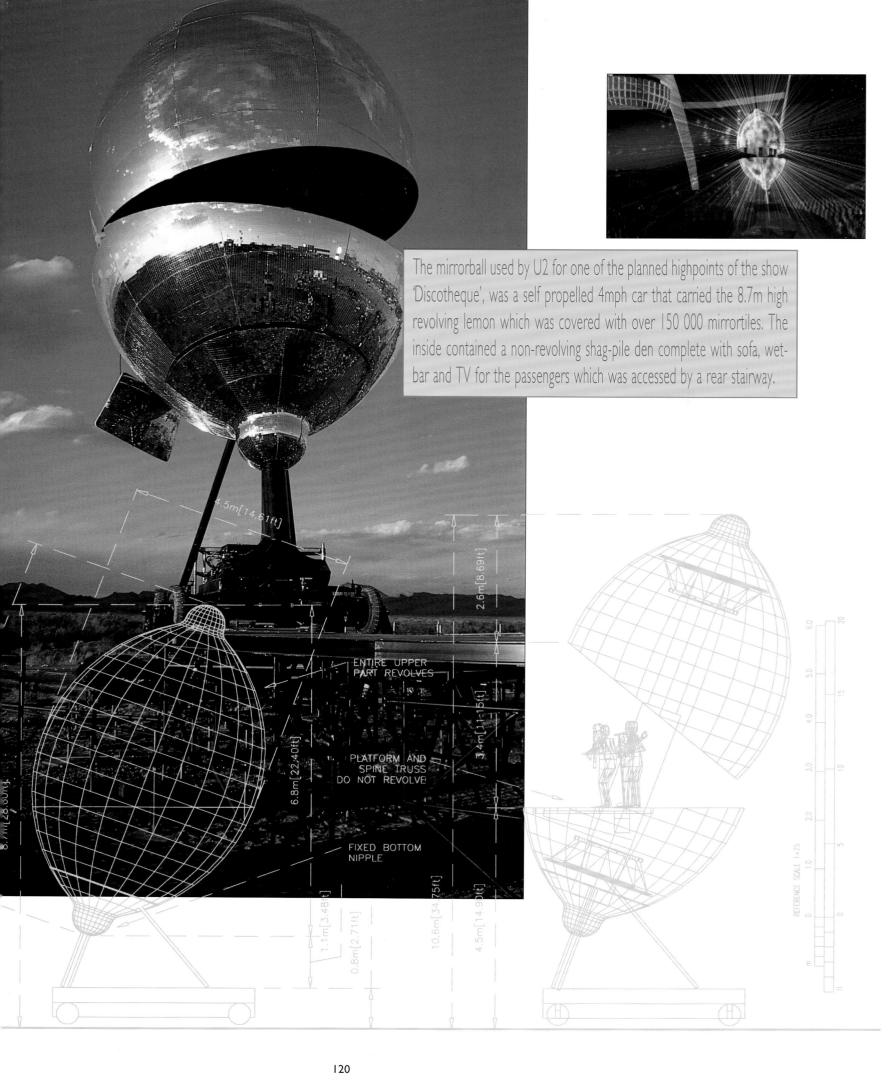

The mirrorball used by U2 for one of the planned highpoints of the show 'Discotheque', was a self propelled 4mph car that carried the 8.7m high revolving lemon which was covered with over 150 000 mirrortiles. The inside contained a non-revolving shag-pile den complete with sofa, wet-bar and TV for the passengers which was accessed by a rear stairway.

4.5m[14.61ft]

2.6m[8.69ft]

3.4m[11.15ft]

ENTIRE UPPER PART REVOLVES

PLATFORM AND SPINE TRUSS DO NOT REVOLVE

FIXED BOTTOM NIPPLE

6.8m[22.40ft]

8.7m[28.80ft]

1.1m[3.48ft]

0.8m[2.71ft]

10.6m[34.75ft]

4.5m[14.90ft]

REFERENCE SCALE 1=75

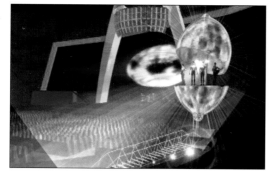  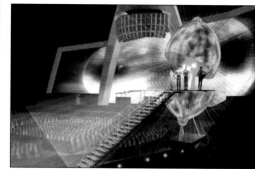

Owens discovered that some of the most interesting work was being carried out in London by a number of young animators using old school painted cell techniques. One of these, Run Wrake, was commissioned to work with the legendary Pop artist Roy Lichtenstein, and they created animated sequences out of several of Lichtenstein's most famous images, including *Whaaam!*, *As I opened fire*, *Takka takka* and *Live Ammo*. The 73-year-old artist was so impressed with the results that he attended the U2 show at the New York Giants Stadium, and Wrake carried out a similar exercise in collaboration with the Estate of Keith Haring, bringing to life the late artist's graffiti-inspired imagery. This 'lo-fi' aesthetic was continued in other material used in the show including the satirical evolution diagram created by Straw Donkey which demonstrated man's development from ape to a shopping-trolley pushing consumer.

Despite the spectacular effects created by the use of the video wall, both Fisher and Williams were aware that on occasion it needed to be 'rested' or de-emphasised in order to give the audience a respite. This was addressed in two very different ways. The first of these concerned the use of a series of low key computer graphics entitled the 'Telecine Baggage Loops', which were made for 'ZooTV' by Brian Eno, and which were played during songs or whilst Bono talked to the audience. The second approach was diametrically opposed to this quiet technique, and involved the use of a 12-metre high glass and aluminium lemon designed by Fisher, which revolved to produce a stunning mirrorball effect. This absurd form also acted as a vehicle, moving across the auditorium to a small second stage where it opened to reveal the band in a sea of dry ice.

The top half of the lemon was fitted with a separate revolve and raise mechanism that was used for the 'reveal'. The passengers exited down a 4.5m high polished alloy staircase which was stored under the in the stage under a sliding cover.

The Popmart tour features the worlds biggest TV screen which was created out of 150 000 pixels with over 1 000 000 separate LED's. The stage contained over 500 tons of equipment including 600 moving lights and a 1 000 000 amps PA system. Approximately 5 000 000 people saw the show generating ticket sales of ......

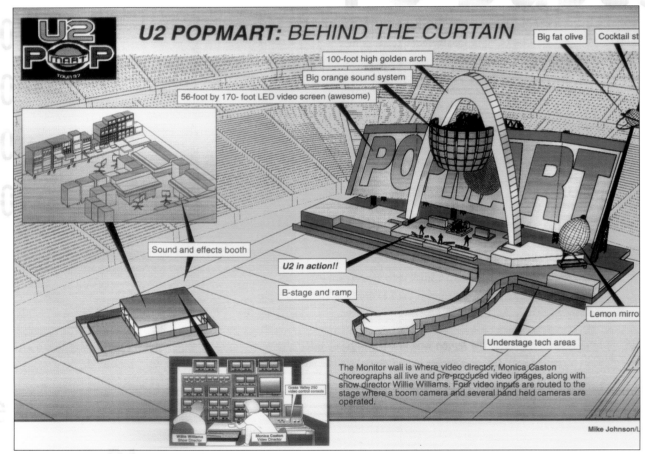

U2 POPMART: BEHIND THE CURTAIN

Big fat olive

Cocktail st

100-foot high golden arch

Big orange sound system

56-foot by 170- foot LED video screen (awesome)

Sound and effects booth

U2 in action!!

B-stage and ramp

Understage tech areas

Lemon mirro

The Monitor wall is where video director, Monica Caston choreographs all live and pre-produced video images, along with show director Willie Williams. Four video inputs are routed to the stage where a boom camera and several hand held cameras are operated.

Willie Williams Show Director

Monica Caston Video Director

Grass Valley 250 video control console

Mike Johnson/L

Boosterism

The irony of beginning the 'Popmart' tour in Las Vegas, the self-styled world capital of consumer excess, and mediated urban space par excellence, was not lost on the band. On the opening night of the show Bono related his own surreal experience of this heavily thematised place by telling the 38,000 crowd '......I woke up this morning in a Pyramid and looked out at the Manhatten skyline - Viva Las Vegas!'. and went on to suggest that 'This is the only town where they're not going to notice a 40ft lemon'. Indeed, Willie Williams himself has recounted that it was not until the road crew reassembled the performance environment in San Diego that he and Fisher realised exactly how outrageous it was.

This notion of excess, which was parodied by the show, has been shown by Simon Frith to have long played an important role in the evaluation of popular entertainment by its audience. Using value judgements drawn from cinema goers in the 1940's, Frith demonstrates in 'Performing Rites' that these frequently drew on the expense incurred in production as a mark of its worth, resulting in 'cheapness' being used as a term of abuse, and the 'spectacular' being assigned a valuable status. He continues by stating that this situation arose due to the fact that 'Audiences expected that their role as consumers would be taken seriously', and that as a consequence, 'American films were constantly rated more highly than British ones...because they took movie goers more seriously in terms of trouble taken (and costs run up)'. Frith concludes by pointing out that 'Hollywood has always been aware of this attitude, of course', and that 'boasting about how much a film has cost is a routine part of the marketing process'.

As a branch of popular entertainment similarly dependant upon a mass audience, rock performance, like cinema, also draws upon the excesses of its production for the marketing its product. This is clearly demonstrated in the 'boosterism' employed in advance publicity materials which exploits remarkable statistical or numerical facts as a way of engaging with its potential audience, and providing conclusive evidence that this is, indeed, a spectacle that demands to be seen.

The physical size of elements of the show, potential audience attendance, production costs, transportation logistics, ticket and merchandising sales are all invoked in this 'boosterist' fascination with excess, and find their way, courtesy of the ubiquitous factsheet, into media coverage of the event. As with cinema, these facts and figures make for good editorial copy as they fill in for an absence, conveying the enormity of spectacle either before it has happened, or without recourse to visual material. Boosterism is not a new phenomena, but can be seen as a contemporary form of showmanship: the art of exhibiting a production to its best advantage. Fisher points out however, that there is a paradox at work in the use of these figures, in that far from demonstrating the uniqueness of an individual rock performance, they are practically identical for every major show.

> Boosterism is a marketing approach that exploits remarkable statistical facts as a way of engaging with its potential audience. Such facts and figures convey the enormity of the spectacle before it has happened and belong to the established tradition of showmanship: the art of exhibiting a performance to its best advantage.

000 000
000 000
000 000
000 000
000 000
000 000

THE EVER INCREASING LEVEL
OF EXCESS UPON WHICH
ROCK SHOWS DEPEND
FOR THEIR IMPACT
RAISES THE QUESTION
AS TO WHETHER
OR NOT AN ENDGAME
IS IN SIGHT FOR
THIS CULTURAL
PHENOMENON

Aftermath

Whilst spectacular live events such as the 'Division Bell', 'Bridges to Babylon' and 'Popmart' have undoubtedly elevated the rock show to new heights in terms of audience experience, the ever increasing level of excess upon which they depend for their impact raises the question as to whether or not an endgame is in sight for this cultural phenomenon. One major factor in this debate appears to be a decrease in the number of bands that can afford the huge financial investment required to take a large show on tour and guarantee the size of audience that will make it viable.

To some extent this situation can be understood within a historical context. It has already been shown that the audience for rock music was generated out of the specific set of social and economic circumstances that gave rise to the baby-boom generation and created a specific market for 'youth culture'. However, the mass appeal of rock bands like The Rolling Stones and Pink Floyd can be attributed to the fact that in the 1960s and early 1970s far fewer groups existed than today and the most successful of these gained a high degree of market penetration for their products. As these groups have matured, their audience has tended to remain loyal, whilst a younger generation of fans has been added to their ranks to create the huge demand for live product that is vital to the staging of a major spectacle.

In contrast, contemporary popular music has been subjected to considerable market fragmentation, with an increasing number of bands engaged in a wider range of musical genres. These not only include straightforward categories such as Rap, Indie, House, Hip Hop, Techno, and Ambient music, but also a myriad of specialised sub-genres such as Jungle, Drum 'n' Bass, Trip Hop, Goa Trance, and Gangsta Rap. As a consequence, the audience for popular music is becoming diffused and less predisposed towards the kind of mass adulation previously experienced by The Rolling Stones. In addition, the products of popular music are having to operate in an increasingly competitive entertainment market, with rock shows vying for audience leisure time with sport, theme parks and multiplexs, and recorded music with computer games, videos and special interest magazines.

Whilst such factors effectively limit the number of bands that can produce live spectacles, the younger bands that do command a substantial audience, such as Oasis, appear to resist this approach to live performance. This attitude can be seen as a part of the same concern with 'authenticity' exhibited by U2 prior to ZooTv. In this mindset the rock spectacle is seen as part of the establishment against which a group needs to rebel in order to resist commodification. In reality, this condition is inescapable given that the popular music industry is predicated on market economics. This is apparent in the 'Indie' music scene to which many of these bands belong, which originally emerged from small independant labels, but it is now essentially financed and marketed by the same large corporations that represent more established acts.

Before reaching any premature conclusions regarding the future of the rock show, it is important to note that, like all cultural production, the development of popular music cannot be read as a linear sequence of events in which musical forms, techniques or approaches to live performance become redundant. Instead creativity can be seen to operate in cyclical time, with society's voracious appetite for fashion giving rise to a constant reworking of older ideas for a new generation of consumers.

The infamous British 'Summer of Love' of 1988 is a testament to this process, when a new generation of youth discovered for themselves the psychedelic music and drug-fuelled hedonism of 1967. The spontaneous acid house 'raves' that took place around the country recalled the events and happenings of the late 1960s. As in the early days of popular music, this phenomenon depended on new technologies, with the electric guitar and TV replaced by the synthesiser, digital sampler and the mobile phone, which was used to relay details of illegal rave venues.

Whilst the 'Summer of Love' appeared to be driven from the street upwards, these creative cycles can also be made to occur from the top down. Simon Frith has related how the popular music industry has long exploited nostalgia as a powerful marketing device, with recorded music being deleted and then re-released after a few years as 'classics'. This technique works by appealing to the memories of individuals for whom important life events are often located in time by contemporaneous records.

The forces of both fashion and nostalgia can be seen in operation in one of Fisher's most recent projects, a concert celebrating the 30th anniversary of Woodstock which took place in the summer of 1999 at an airbase in New York State. The marketing material for this event was a triumph of boosterism, which promoted the event under the commodified hippy-speak of 'Uniting the Generations'. This not only targeted the aging baby boomers for whom Woodstock represented a cultural landmark inextricably tied to their youth, but also the children

of this generation who wished to experience it for themselves.

Fisher saw a great irony in being commissioned as the 'Masterplanner' for this event, and having to apply the logic of urban planning to an ephemeral event that covered 1200 acres and created a temporary city the size of Cannes. In its conception, the project proved cyclical even for Fisher himself who returned to the notions of Archigrams's 'Instant City' project of 1970, which itself had been influenced by the first Woodstock festival in 1969.

Given the strength of the commercial forces and audience desire driving events like Woodstock, it would appear that the rock show as a cultural phenomenon will continue its evolution into ever more spectacular events.

This of course leaves the rock show industry facing the challenge of how to surpass the kinds of reckless extravaganzas illustrated in this book, in a world where, to quote the title of Morris Lapidus' autobiography, 'Too much is never enough'. It might find some inspiration in the words of Jean Cocteau, who once suggested, 'There is only one thing to do when you have gone too far....... and that's to go further.'

'THERE IS ONLY ONE
THING TO DO
WHEN YOU
HAVE GONE
TOO FAR AND
THAT'S
TO GO
FURTHER'

Playlist
(a Selected Bibliography)

Books

J Baudrillard, *Simulations*, Semiotext(e) (New York), 1983.

S Bukatman, *Bladerunner*, British Film Institute (London), 1997.

I Chambers, *Popular Culture: The Metropolitan Experience*, Routledge (London), 1986.

I Chambers, *Urban Rhythms: Pop Music and Popular Culture*, McMillan (Oxford), 1988.

S Chaplin and E Holding, *Consuming Architecture*, Academy Editions (London), 1998.

S Conolly, M Davis, J Devas, D Harrison and D Martin, 'Pneu World', *Architectural Design* (London), 1969.

P Cook, *Experimental Architecture*, Studio Vista (London), 1970.

P Cook (ed), *Archigram*, Birkhäuser Verlag (Berlin), 1991.

M Düttmann and F Schneider, *Morris Lapidus: Architect of the American Dream*, Birkhäuser Verlag (Berlin), 1992.

S Frith, *Sound Effects: Youth, Leisure and the Politics of Rock 'n' Roll*, Constable (London), 1983.

S Frith, *Performing Rites,* Oxford University Press (Oxford), 1996.

M Gottdiener, *The Theming of America*, Westview Press (Boulder), 1997.

D Hebdige, *Subculture: The Meaning of Style*, Methuen (London), 1987.

D Hebdige, *Hiding in the Light*, Routledge (London), 1988.

R Kronenburg, *Portable Architecture*, Architectural Press (Oxford), 1996.

S Lyall, *Rock Sets: The Astonishing Art of Rock Concert Design,* Thames & Hudson (London), 1992.

A Schönberger (ed), *Raymond Loewy: Pioneer of American Industrial Design*, Prestel-Verlag (Munich), 1990.

S Thorgerson, *Mind over matter: The images of Pink Floyd*, Sanctuary Publishing (London), 1997.

Articles

P Arcidi, 'Timely adjustments: retrofit technology', article in *Architectural Design,* Volume 60, Issue 3/4, 1990.

N Coates, 'Street signs', article in John Thakara (ed), *Design after Modernism*, Thames & Hudson (London), 1988.

B Curtis, 'Archigram – A Necessary Irritant', article in D Crompton, *Concerning Archigram*, Archigram Archives (London), 1998.

S Dawson, 'All the World's a Stage', article in *Architects Journal,* 10 July 1997.

M Fisher, 'Design for Entertainment', article in *British Architecture*, Academy Editions (London), 1982.

M Fisher, 'It's only Rock 'n' Roll: The Steel Wheels American Tour', article in *Architectural Design,* Volume 60, Issue 3/4, 1990.

J Fiske, 'Popular Discrimination', article in J Navemore & P Brantlinger (eds), *Modernity and Mass Culture*, Indiana University Press, 1991.

T Gottelier and D Loth, 'The Rolling Stones Voodoo Lounge Tour', article in *Lighting and Sound International,* September 1994.

L Grossberg, 'The Media Economy of Rock Culture', article in S Frith and L Grossberg (eds), *Sound and Vision,* Routledge (London), 1993.

P Leigh Brown, 'Guerilla Architecture: The Stones Set,' article in *International Herald Tribune,* 7/8 October 1989.

C Melhuish, 'Go to work on a silvery egg', article in *Building Design Magazine*, 23 May 1997.

K Rattenbury, 'Lights, Music, Action,' article in *Building Design,* 17 February 1995.

D Redhead, 'Shopping all over the World', article in *Daily Telegraph*, 19 April 1997.

S Rushdie, 'The armies of pleasure', article in *The Observer,* 16 July 1995.

M Sorkin, 'Introduction', article taken from D Crompton, *Concerning Archigram*, Archigram Archives (London), 1998.

S Smith, 'The Fly on the Stage: Readings and Misreadings of the "New U2", paper presented to The Popular Culture Association.

Except as noted below, all sketches, drawings, colour illustrations and photographs are by Mark Fisher. All computer renderings and video animation frames are by Adrian Mudd at the Mark Fisher Studio.

p9 Urban Salon, p10–15 Martin Tothill, p16 UPI/Bettmann Archive, p18 TL & TC Mike Davies, TR Jeffrey Shaw, p19 Archigram, p21 AD Magazine, p23 TL Jon Hardy, BR AD Magazine, p33–34 Richard Bentley, Atelier One Ltd, p46 Paul Slattery/Retna, p47 TL Paul Slattery/Retna, TR Mick Treadwell, p48 Jarre Graphics, 4i Limited, Houston photo, Jean-Michel Jarre, p49 Guardian Archive, p50–51 Alberto Lopes, p92–93 Steel Wheels – Francis Chee, U2 ZooTV – Mark Fisher and Jonathan Park, Voodoo Lounge – Mark Fisher and Jonathan Park, p106 Richard Bentley, Atelier One Ltd.